PRAISE FOR
THE HEALED HEART

"*The Healed Heart* by Joel Vaught is a wonderful read for anyone seeking to find healing and freedom from addiction. Through his personal experiences and reflections on Scripture, Joel provides readers with a powerful companion along their personal journey in recovery... Whether you are currently on a recovery journey or know someone who is, *The Healed Heart* is a great resource. It is a beacon of hope and a testament to the transformative power of God's love."

— Brant C., Pastor and TRF Coach

"Throughout the book, [Joel's] unique voice shines through... I think the book has content beneficial for all believers as [Joel takes] us deeper into knowing the heart of the Father and his intent for us."

— Julian S., Worship Leader and TRF Graduate

THE
HEALED
HEART

THE HEALED HEART

90 DAYS TO REDISCOVERING YOUR
IDENTITY, LIFE, AND MISSION IN CHRIST

JOEL VAUGHT

To Pastors Greg and Lisa,
Words can't fully describe your impact on me.
Your love, grace, and leadership changed my life.
I wouldn't be the man I am today without you.

INTRODUCTION

"We are not called to be comfortable but to obedience."
Paul Alverson, Chick-fil-A Operator

"**N**o matter what it takes, no matter the cost, I'm going to give this a shot." These were the words that I told myself when I went into my initial interview for *The Retention Formula* (TRF). I had no idea what I was getting into. It was my first ever Zoom meeting, and I had never been so open about my struggles with porn, masturbation, and orgasm (PMO) with another person before. But after 22 years, I knew something had to change to find freedom.

I was first exposed to the evils of pornography when I was 11 years old. While I was on a Boy Scouts camping trip in middle school, some peers ridiculed me because I had never seen a naked woman before. These high schoolers seemed so cool, and here I was, a self-conscious, nerdy kid desperately trying to find my place in the world. They all laughed in unison at my innocence. Their mocking cut deeply to my soul.

I longed desperately for acceptance. Up to that point in my life, I had a difficult time finding and keeping friends. I was teased, picked on, and bullied often by my classmates in school and after-school programs. On top of that, my parents had recently divorced, leaving me to split my weeks between a hardworking and caring father and an increasingly absent mother. Rejection had become commonplace in my life from my "friends" and my mother especially, so I reached out for love and acceptance however I could. After that camping trip, I decided that I was going to be like one of those cool high schoolers. I stayed up late the night I returned home and did a quick internet search once everyone else was asleep. It didn't take long to find a pornographic website. I was hooked.

For the next several years, I couldn't get away from it. I stayed up late most nights to steal as much time as I could online. Soon, masturbation was incorporated, and the cocktail of chemicals rushing through my body was intoxicating to my juvenile mind. I became obsessed; it was all I could think about. It's what I lived for.

Something shifted in my life when I was 13 years old. My aunt told me about this youth group at her church that was starting a praise band. Since I was in the symphonic band in school, she urged me to join them and play my trumpet in their band. I was introduced to a newlywed couple in their early 20s who were the leaders of the group. They would soon introduce me to Jesus. I knew about God and Jesus and the Bible, but this couple, along with their parents, introduced me to the God of the Bible—the God who loved me and wanted a real relationship with me. I gave my life to Christ one night while I was alone in my bedroom after I realized I needed to be saved.

For the next several years, I grew to love the Lord. I attended church faithfully and got involved with everything I could. In fact, my sister and I were considered the "black sheep" of the youth group because we were trying to pursue God instead of a social club. It was a wonderful time.

But the chains of pornography were still there.

My addiction to PMO didn't get any better. In fact, it got worse! Before, I would consume pornography, and it didn't faze me. Now, suddenly, I could feel the weight of my sin. What I was OK with before no longer felt good. Afterwards, I would always felt guilty and ashamed. I felt condemned and like a hypocrite. "What kind of Christian is OK with looking at this stuff?" I would ask myself. My questions felt like they were hitting deaf ears as the addiction continued to grip me.

In my junior year of high school, I was invited by my girlfriend at the time to attend a Wednesday night service at her church. I accepted without hesitation, and I'm glad that I did. That service was designed by God for me. The presence of the Holy Spirit was so strong as I sang along with a setlist made up entirely of familiar songs, and I connected immediately with the adults and other teenagers there. Two weeks later, I found myself at their Friday night youth group service where I encountered the presence of the Holy Spirit in a way I would never forget. The rush I felt from PMO had nothing on this. I wanted as much of the Lord that I could get.

It was during this season I gave my life completely and wholeheartedly to Christ. I loved God before, but now I wanted to give my life in complete service to him. My life completely changed.

I was filled and empowered by the Holy Spirit. I wanted to read the Bible more and be in praise and worship as much as possible. If I could be at church, I would be there. Anything I could do to be with God, I wanted to do it.

But the chains of pornography were still there.

The guilt I experienced before was now magnified ten-fold. I longed for God with all of my being, and yet I felt trapped. I sought counseling from my pastor and friends, and I read books on sexual freedom and purity. As a result, I would experience *some* periods of freedom... only to fall right back on my face. I was the proverbial dog continually returning to its vomit.[1]

I was utterly miserable. Trapped. Ashamed.

One night at a church prayer meeting, the Holy Spirit spoke clearly to me and called me to preach, pastor, and plant new churches. I felt an urgency to teach God's Word and serve him in full-time ministry. So, I forfeited my full-ride scholarship at a local university to pursue Eagle Summit Academy, a small Bible school and internship my pastors created just for me and eight others who also felt called to ministry. For the next two years, I devoted my life to studying the Bible and serving the Church. My heart was determined to be used by God to fulfill what he had called me to do. As a result, I experienced the greatest strides of freedom and victory in my entire life.

But the chains of pornography were still there.

After graduating from Bible school, the other graduates and I were transitioned from being interns to having active roles on the church's ministry team. I led kids church teams. I served on the worship team and was part of the youth leadership. When given the privilege to preach a Sunday morning service or lead a Bible study or class, I zealously took the opportunity. I even began to regularly preach chapel services at our local Adult & Teen Challenge, a faith-based rehabilitation program for men seeking freedom from addiction. I was doing what I was called to do, and I felt the most alive doing these things. I did everything that I could to be pure before God before ever standing in the pulpit. Leading up to a church service to preach or serve, I fasted, prayed, worshiped, and committed myself to God. I wanted to do what was right.

But the chains of pornography were still there.

I didn't understand! How could I have known so much truth and still be bound? How could I have preached sermons about abstaining from sexual sin and living a holy life but be continually drawn to pornography? How could I stand before my friends, family, and church and act like everything was OK, when my soul was crying out for help? I felt like the Apostle Paul:

"I don't really understand myself, for I want to do what is right, but I don't do it. Instead, I do what I hate... I want to do what is right, but I can't. I want to do what is good, but I don't. I don't want to do what is wrong, but I do it anyway. But if I do what I don't want to do, I am not really the one doing wrong; it is sin living in me that does it. I have discovered this principle of life—that when I want to do what is right, I inevitably do what is wrong... Oh, what a miserable person I am! Who will free me from this life that is dominated by sin and death?"[2]

5

On May 5, 2022, I had reached a breaking point. I cried out to God for the millionth time for deliverance from this sin eating away at my soul. I needed to be free. The next day after this desperate prayer, I received a "random" direct message from Gianfranco Martinez, founder of *The Retention Formula*, a coaching program and community designed to help men overcome PMO addiction. I had been following his page on Instagram for a while, and the content Gianfranco regularly posted was entertaining and encouraging.

I mentioned this briefly to him and that I had struggled with PMO for a long time. That's when he cut to the chase: "How long have you been struggling with this?" So, I told a total stranger what I had been keeping inside for so long: I had a pull towards pornography that I could not shake, and I was ready to be done. For good.

"No matter what it takes, no matter the cost, I'm going to give this a shot."

I joined TRF a few days later after that Zoom interview. During this program, I made practical lifestyle changes like cutting out social media, gray scaling my phone, getting up earlier every day, and taking cold showers. I watched teaching material, did homework, and read a couple of books. One change that I made was returning to having an early morning devotion every day. First thing every morning, I sat down at my kitchen table to read the Bible and pray. I also decided to incorporate journaling during these devotions. Even though it had been a long time since I had journaled, I quickly got back into the flow of writing down my thoughts and prayers while I read the Bible. As the days progressed, the Holy Spirit revealed truth after truth that revolutionized my thinking and how I lived.

This book is a collection of those devotions during my 90-day journey of freedom through *The Retention Formula*. The layout of each day is very simple. You will find a passage of Scripture to read followed by a specific verse to reflect on. Then, I'll give some applications and observations I made from the text. I conclude each day with a prayer that you can agree with for your own life.

Are you struggling with overcoming pornography? Have guilt, shame, and condemnation consumed your mind and left you feeling like a shell of who you know you're supposed to be? I invite you to journey with me as I rediscovered my identity, life, and mission in Christ. My prayer is that these reflections on God's Word will transform your mind and soul like they did for me. On the following page is the initial prayer from my journal. Make it yours as you begin your journey of freedom and to a healed heart.

God, I dedicate the next 90 days to you. Speak to me powerfully as you heal my physical mind and my spiritual soul. As I read your Word, transform me into a new person—one who no longer desires PMO and only desires the things that please you. In Jesus' name, amen!

"And so, dear brothers and sisters, I plead with you to give your bodies to God because of all he has done for you. Let them be a living and holy sacrifice—the kind he will find acceptable. This is truly the way to worship him. Don't copy the behavior and customs of this world, but let God transform you into a new person by changing the way you think. Then you will learn to know God's will for you, which is good and pleasing and perfect."

Romans 12:1–2

Knowledge alone won't produce lasting change. Circumstances and feelings will eventually dictate how you live. But when knowledge drops to your heart, it becomes a conviction— a standard of living. Show me a man who is unwavering, and I'll show you a man with deep convictions.

DAY 1

GOD CHOSE ME!

READ: GALATIANS 1

"But even before I was born, God chose me and called me by his marvelous grace. Then it pleased him to reveal his Son to me so that I would proclaim the Good News about Jesus to the Gentiles."

Galatians 1:15–16

God chose me! He called me! I'm not anything special. I have all kinds of problems: addictions to break, emotions to heal, and mindsets to shift. But even before any of these problems developed in my life, God chose me! And the amazing thing is that he wanted to! It gave him great pleasure to choose me to be a part of his family.

God called me! I remember the calling God placed on my life. He called me so that I could join him in the work he is doing around me. I also know part of God's calling for my life is to share my victories with other people. This journey of freedom *will* help others experience freedom in their own lives. My testimony *will* be powerful and many *will* come to know the Lord from hearing it. It's amazing how God chooses and calls imperfect people to accomplish his purposes. He can use me to fulfill his plans!

———————◆•◆•◆———————

Lord, thank you for revealing your son, Jesus, to me. Thank you for choosing me to be a part of your family and involved in your mission to reconcile this world back to you. Thank you for giving me a purpose by calling me to spread the Good News to others. Holy Spirit, fill me with the strength I need to live out this mission!

DAY 2
GRACE

READ: GALATIANS 2

"Yet we know that a person is made right with God by faith in Jesus Christ, not by obeying the law... For when I tried to keep the law, it condemned me. So I died to the law—I stopped trying to meet all its requirements—so that I might live for God... I do not treat the grace of God as meaningless. For if keeping the law could make us right with God, then there was no need for Christ to die."

Galatians 2:16, 19, 21

Right standing with God is not based on what I do; it is solely based on faith in Jesus Christ. Therefore, because I have faith in Jesus Christ, I have been made right with God. God no longer holds my sins against me. I am forgiven! The debt has been paid! I didn't do anything to deserve God's grace, and there is nothing that I must do to *continue* to earn God's grace either. Whether I follow all the things I am "supposed" to do as a Christian doesn't change his love for me.

Keeping endless rules doesn't make me right with God. It's only by God's grace I'm saved!

There must be a mindset shift. I don't want to obey God because I feel pressured or obligated. I want to obey God because I love him. My desire for obedience must stem from a love for God. I didn't earn grace when I first received it, so I don't have to work to keep it. Grace is, and will always be, free and undeserved.

———————◆•◆•◆———————

Thank you, God, for your amazing grace! It truly is free and undeserved. I receive your grace fresh and new in my life today. Help me to want to obey you every single day! Forgive me where my Christian walk has turned into duty. I want to follow and obey you out of a heart of love and gratitude.

DAY 3
NO LONGER A SLAVE

READ: GALATIANS 3:1-4:7

"But the Scriptures declare that we are all prisoners of sin, so we receive God's promise of freedom only by believing in Jesus Christ... God sent him to buy freedom for us who were slaves to the law, so that he could adopt us as his very own children... Now you are no longer a slave but God's own child. And since you are his child, God has made you his heir."

Galatians 3:22; 4:5, 7

What a glorious and amazing promise! If I relate this to the PMO-free journey, the Word declares that I was once a slave to it. I was PMO's prisoner. As a prisoner and slave, I must do what my master commands. Every whim, every call to action, every single command must be completed. For I have no say or opinion when I am a slave.

But God! He sent Jesus to rescue me. He sent Jesus to set me free from the bondages of PMO and sexual sin. He didn't buy me out of slavery with money. No, he bought me with his own life. He died so I could be released from my sin, addiction, and hurts. Now that I have faith in Christ and have accepted this freedom, I am no longer tied to the old master of sin. Now I can walk in freedom! Now I live, not as a slave, but as a child of God. Now I am a part of his family—loved and accepted for who I am!

———————◆◆◆———————

Lord, I choose today to believe that it is by your grace I am free from all my sins. I choose to continually walk in your freedom. Help my mind shift from dwelling on guilt, fear, and shame to remembering your goodness and grace. Empower me, Holy Spirit, to stand firm in who I am in Christ Jesus. Thank you for freedom!

DAY 4
WHY GO BACK?

READ: GALATIANS 4:8-31

"So now that you know God (or should I say, now that God knows you), why do you want to go back again and become slaves once more to the weak and useless spiritual principles of this world?"

Galatians 4:9

Why would I want to go back to the old life and become a slave again? Why would I want to go back to PMO when Jesus has set me free from a jail cell of guilt, shame, and condemnation? Is a fleeting pleasure worth the consequences of being back in bondage to sin?

No.

When I think about the negative effects PMO gives me, the lies are exposed clearer than ever. PMO is a waste of time. It kills me physically, mentally, and emotionally. It robs me of joy. It pours shame and guilt into my heart. It poisons my mind into thinking that my family and friends don't love me. PMO makes me insecure in who I am. It makes me look differently at those I care about. PMO makes me view women as sexual objects instead of people made in the image of God. Why would I *ever* want to go back to any of this?

—————————◆•◆•◆—————————

Father, thank you for this question today. It's a question that I greatly needed. I ask that you help me remember these negative consequences when temptations arise. Help me to focus more on the positive consequences of freedom: love, acceptance, security, a clear and pure mind, and a closer relationship with you. Your love far outweighs any perceived pleasure associated with PMO. The love of my friends and family far outweighs the high of PMO. God, please continue to renew my mind. I want to be all that you want me to be.

DAY 5
TRULY FREE

READ: GALATIANS 5

"So Christ has truly set us free. Now make sure that you stay free, and don't get tied up again in slavery to the law... For you have been called to live in freedom, my brothers and sisters. But don't use your freedom to satisfy your sinful nature. Instead, use your freedom to serve one another in love."

Galatians 5:1 ,13

I have truly been set free! "In [this] freedom Christ has made us free [and completely liberated us]."[1] Sin used to be my slave master. I was always under its whim to run to PMO to do what my flesh desired. I was masking the real issues and needs in my life. This resulted in me continually putting on a "yoke of slavery."[2] But Christ has set me free! I am not in bondage any longer. Sin has no power over me![3] The passions and evil desires of my flesh died on the cross with Jesus.[4] I now identify with his resurrection power and undeserved grace in me.

I have been called to freedom. So where do I expend the time and energy that I used to put into PMO? Paul's encouragement is to "serve one another in love."

Lord, thank you for freedom! I refuse to return to the slavery and bondages of PMO and my selfish desires. I choose to worship you by being a living sacrifice—holy and pleasing to you.[5] I want to take this newly discovered time and energy to serve others in love. I want to love those around me the best that I can. Holy Spirit, help me to do just that.

DAY 6
MY OWN WORK

READ: GALATIANS 6:1-6

"Pay careful attention to your own work, for then you will get the satisfaction of a job well done, and you won't need to compare yourself to anyone else."

Galatians 6:4

When it comes to the Christian life, far too often I have compared what I am doing with what others have done. I tend to look at how other people are walking with the Lord. Do I pray as long? Do I read as much of the Bible? Other times I am comparing my performance in serving the Lord with how others serve God. She reads these books, so that means I should too. He is listening to those podcasts, so I need to as well. The list of examples is endless!

But Paul says that I should "pay careful attention to [my] own work."[1] What has God called *me* to do? Sure, the things I "should" do are noble and good for my walk with Christ, but what has the Holy Spirit asked of me? Who and what should I be praying for? What should I be studying in the Bible? Where has God called me to serve faithfully? What assignments has he given me? God is concerned about me fulfilling my own work—what he has called me to do and who he has called me to be.

God, forgive me for where I have been focusing too much on what others are doing instead of focusing on what you have called me to do. Forgive me for emulating someone else when you have called me to be me. I want to pay careful attention to my own work, not the work of others. I want to experience the satisfaction that comes when I hear you say, "Well done, good and faithful servant."[2]

DAY 7
DON'T GIVE UP
READ: GALATIANS 6:7-18

"So let's not get tired of doing what is good.
At just the right time we will reap a harvest
of blessing if we don't give up."

Galatians 6:9

The Apostle Paul issues the wake-up call: What I sow, that's what I'll reap. This is a principle embedded throughout the world. If I plant apple seeds, then an apple tree will grow. If I plant corn, then corn will grow. I can't expect cucumbers to grow when I plant tomatoes. It works the same in spiritual matters. If I live for my sinful flesh, then corruption *will* be harvested. This happened in the past with PMO. I planted those seeds of lust and immorality, and as a result, I reaped a harvest of unchecked desires and addiction. The fruits of my fleshly harvest were guilt, shame, condemnation, and bondage.

But if I live for God, then I will harvest things that bring me closer to God and develop maturity into my life. If I don't give up planting good seeds in my life, then I *will* reap a harvest of blessing. I will experience peace, love, and joy in my life. I will feel fulfilled in life and move closer to God. My emotions will be steady, and my relationships with others will improve. That's why I can't give up. I can't back down.

——◆•◆•◆——

Father, I have been sowing to the flesh for far too long, and the results are clear. Forgive me for the evil things I have planted and harvested in my life. I choose today to plant good things into my life so I can harvest godliness. I commit to not giving up any longer in doing good. I will reap a harvest of freedom!

DAY 8
FLOODED WITH LIGHT
READ: EPHESIANS 1

"I pray that your hearts will be flooded with light
so that you can understand the confident hope
he has given to those he called—his holy people
who are his rich and glorious inheritance."

Ephesians 1:18

P aul prays my heart would be "flooded with light." How is my heart filled with light? It's through hearing and knowing the truth. Paul lists at least five truths about who I am in Christ: Because I am in Christ, I am blessed with every spiritual blessing.[1] God loved me and chose me to be holy and blameless in his sight.[2] Through Christ, God chose to adopt me into his own family.[3] Because I united with Christ, I have received an inheritance from God,[4] and the guarantee of my eternal inheritance is that I am sealed by his Holy Spirit.[5]

These are amazing declarations of how God sees me and who I really am. To become the best version of myself, I must understand and accept who I truly am now that I belong to Christ. How I perceive myself is how I will live out my life. Therefore, I must see myself how God sees me.

Thank you, God, for showing and reminding me of the freedom I have in you. You are reminding me of who I truly am! Flood my heart with light! Holy Spirit, help me to fully understand this hope. I ask that you continually remind me of these truths. Help them be in the forefront of my thoughts. Thank you for your grace, love, and power within me.

DAY 9
BEFORE AND AFTER

READ: EPHESIANS 2

"You lived in this world without God and without hope. But now you have been united with Christ Jesus. Once you were far away from God, but now you have been brought near to him through the blood of Christ."
Ephesians 2:12–13

I used to be dead. I lived like the world and was led by my flesh and the devil. I pursued passionate desires. My will was bent towards every little impulse to fulfill my lust. I was filled with guilt, regret, and shame. I believed I was living, but I was a walking dead man.

The good news is that God is filled with an abundance of kindness and mercy! He loved me even when I was against him. He loved me in my disobedience. Before I ever knew him, God made a way to give me life by sending Jesus to die for my rebellion and sins. He offered me his love and grace.

Because I have accepted Jesus Christ as my Lord and Savior, I am no longer dead. I'm alive! I don't live for the flesh but after Christ and holiness. My will isn't bent towards lustful

29

passions but towards God's supreme will. No longer am I filled with condemnation. Now I'm filled with freedom and peace. Before his grace entered my life, I was dead. Now, I am alive and united with Christ.

———————◆•◆•◆———————

Father, because I have received your grace, I have been transformed into a brand-new person.[1] I am no longer dead. I have come to life! I'm not the man I was. You have changed my identity. So now, Holy Spirit, mold me into the man you have created me to be!

DAY 10
PAUL'S PRAYER

READ: EPHESIANS 3

"I pray that from his glorious, unlimited resources he will empower you with inner strength through his Spirit. Then Christ will make his home in your hearts as you trust in him. Your roots will grow down into God's love and keep you strong. And may you have the power to understand, as all God's people should, how wide, how long, how high, and how deep his love is. May you experience the love of Christ, though it is too great to understand fully. Then you will be made complete with all the fullness of life and power that comes from God. Now all glory to God, who is able, through his mighty power at work within us, to accomplish infinitely more than we might ask or think."

Ephesians 3:16–20

The Apostle Paul's prayer was for believers to experience deep spiritual growth. His desire was for Christians to become complete in Christ, so Paul explained a progression for this growth in my life. The first step is that I need inner strength from the Holy Spirit. Situations are going to come into my life where I will be tested to see if I will trust Christ and grow up spiritually.[1] During these times, I will need the Holy Spirit's strength to allow the roots of Jesus' love to grow deeper. As I experience God's love more, I will be stronger in my faith and full of God's life and power.

———◆———

Father, from your glorious, unlimited resources empower me with inner strength to stay strong and pure. Let my roots grow deeply into your love. Help me to gain a greater understanding and appreciation for your love and grace. Thank you that I am complete in you!

DAY 11
THROW IT OFF
READ: EPHESIANS 4

"With the Lord's authority I say this: Live no longer as the Gentiles do, for they are hopelessly confused... throw off your old sinful nature and your former way of life, which is corrupted by lust and deception. Instead, let the Spirit renew your thoughts and attitudes. Put on your new nature, created to be like God—truly righteous and holy."

Ephesians 4:17, 22–24

This is a clear commandment and admonishment from the Lord: Don't live like the world. I can't live like I used to live. I must throw the old life off! It's corrupted—dirty, musty, holey, grimy, and covered in sweat, dirt, and blood from living a life against God. There is a temptation to carefully take it off, smooth out the wrinkles, and put it back in the closet to be worn another day. But the Apostle Paul said to throw it away! I must get rid of everything connected with the old way of life and put on the new nature. This means that I must continually strive to live a righteous and holy life. I must allow

God to continually renew my thoughts and attitudes. As I do this daily, I will be changed into a new person.[1]

———◆•◆•◆———

God, I choose to throw off the old life and put on the new. The old life was filled with lust and deception, and it brought terrible consequences into my life. I refuse to go back to the old way of living. Instead, I choose to live for you. I ask, Holy Spirit, that you would continue to renew my thoughts and attitudes. Make me into the man you created me to be: "truly righteous and holy."

DAY 12
IMITATE CHRIST

READ: EPHESIANS 5

"Imitate God, therefore, in everything you do, because you are his dear children. Live a life filled with love, following the example of Christ. He loved us and offered himself as a sacrifice for us, a pleasing aroma to God."

Ephesians 5:1–2

Jesus was the most selfless person on earth. He served, loved, and even sacrificed his life for others. Because I have been adopted into his family,1 I should imitate my life after my Father.

So how should I act toward others? Like Christ—imitate him! How should I look at others, especially women? Like Christ—imitate him! How should I think about my life's trials, hurts, and difficulties? Like Christ—imitate him! In every way and in everything I do, my aim should be to imitate Jesus.

The ways of the world are contrary to living like Christ. That's why there is to be "no sexual immorality, impurity, or greed among [me]."2 Because I am a child of God, I need to act like who I really am. No wonder I feel out of place and miserable when I'm allowing sin into my life! It doesn't line up with who I really am!

Father, help me to imitate Jesus in everything that I do! My desire is to live a life full of love, just like you did when you were here on the earth. Show me ways to love, serve, and sacrifice for others, especially those I love and care about the most. Let my life be a living sacrifice continually offered up as a pleasing aroma to you.[3]

DAY 13
A SPIRITUAL BATTLE

READ: EPHESIANS 6

"Put on all of God's armor so that you will be able to stand firm against all strategies of the devil. For we are not fighting against flesh-and-blood enemies, but against evil rulers and authorities of the unseen world, against mighty powers in this dark world, and against evil spirits in the heavenly places."

Ephesians 6:11–12

I am in a spiritual battle. The devil is constantly trying to get me to be busy, sin against God or others, become enslaved to sin, or sit idly and do nothing. The enemy's goal is to steal, kill, and destroy.[1] He will do whatever it takes to ruin my relationship with God and others. There is a spiritual principality behind PMO addiction that had gripped me for so long. This spirit of lust was destroying my life. I attempted to beat such a powerful foe with my own strength and resources, but I continually failed. It's all because I didn't humble myself to receive strength and power from the Holy Spirit!

I can't deny the spiritual war attached to PMO. The devil doesn't want me to be free. He knows my potential, and he is scared. He is worried about who I am in Christ and who I will become to further the Kingdom of God. I recognize that I'm in a spiritual battle. The good news is the war was won by Jesus on the cross. Jesus triumphed over the devil by his victory.[2] I am free in Christ. Equipped with God's armor, I can stand firm to face every battle and challenge thrown my way.

God, thank you for the freedom you have given me. Thank you for rescuing and saving me. I put on the full armor of God so I will not be defeated or outsmarted by the devil and his minions. I line up with your truth and stand firm in your mighty power against the evil forces of darkness seeking to destroy my life. Give me the strength to resist temptation and stand firm against spiritual attacks, for when I resist the devil, he must flee.[3] I submit my life to you, Lord Jesus.

DAY 14
WHAT REALLY MATTERS
READ: PHILIPPIANS 1

"I pray that your love will overflow more and more, and that you will keep on growing in knowledge and understanding. For I want you to understand what really matters, so that you may live pure and blameless lives until the day of Christ's return."

Philippians 1:9–10

The Apostle Paul prayed I would "understand what really matters." There is a motivating force behind everything that I do, so it is vital that my motives are pure. What is it that really matters? According to Paul, it was the Gospel! The Apostle Paul mentions the Gospel at least six times:

"You have been my partners in spreading the Good News about Christ."[1] "You share with me the special favor of God... in defending and confirming the truth of the Good News."[2] "Everything that has happened to me here has helped to spread the Good News."[3] "Because of my imprisonment, most of the believers here have gained confidence and boldly speak God's message without fear."[4] "The message about Christ is being preached."[5] "I will know that you are standing together with one spirit and one purpose, fighting together for the faith, which is the Good News."[6]

It couldn't be more obvious what was most important to Paul. Everything he lived for was centered around sharing the Good News of Jesus dying for the sins of the world. It was Paul's desire for every believer to understand this deeply. As I understand the depth and weight of the Gospel, I desire more and more to live a life that is full of purity and holiness until Jesus returns for his church. There is no greater way to express my gratitude and love!

———◆•◆•◆———

God, help me to understand what really matters in life— the Gospel! I want my love for you and for others to overflow. I ask, Holy Spirit, for you to fill me up with your love and grace. I desire to grow in my knowledge and understanding of who you are. Continually reveal more of yourself to me.

DAY 15
AS CITIZENS OF HEAVEN

READ: PHILIPPIANS 1:27-2:30

"Above all, you must live as citizens of heaven, conducting yourselves in a manner worthy of the Good News about Christ."

Philippians 1:27

This world is not my home. I have a new citizenship—heaven! I am just a temporary resident[1] until I arrive to the home Jesus is preparing for me.[2] Since this world is not my home, I should be conducting myself like the citizen of heaven that I am.

Paul shows me many ways to live as a citizen of heaven: I should stand united together with other believers in one spirit and purpose.[3] I should be agreeable, love, and work together with others.[4] I need to be humble and look to other's interests and needs[5] while having the sacrificial attitude of Christ.[6] I must live a clean and innocent life[7] while I serve in preaching the Gospel.[8] It is a high calling to live as a citizen of heaven in an evil, sinful world. However, this is the only lifestyle to fully exemplify the Good News about Christ.

———————◆•◆•◆———————

Father, thank you for changing my citizenship! I have been transferred from the kingdom of darkness to the kingdom of your dear Son![9] As I live in this sinful world, help me to live my life worthy of the Good News. Give me the grace I need to have the attitude of Jesus in my life. Holy Spirit, empower me to live as a citizen of heaven.

DAY 16
FORGETTING THE PAST
READ: PHILIPPIANS 3

"No, dear brothers and sisters, I have not achieved it, but I focus on this one thing: Forgetting the past and looking forward to what lies ahead, I press on to reach the end of the race and receive the heavenly prize for which God, through Christ Jesus, is calling us."
Philippians 3:13–14

It's tough to forget the past, and the Apostle Paul had a rough one. Before he had his encounter with Jesus, he persecuted the church![1] Paul stood by and watched approvingly as the Jewish leaders killed Stephen![2] When I look back at my life, I've done many things I'm not proud of and wished I had not done. PMO, especially, wasted so much of my life that it pains me to think of what could have been accomplished. The feelings of guilt and shame from wasting so much time can be overwhelming and crippling.

Despite what Paul had done and experienced, he had a single focus: to reach the heavenly prize. He determined that he couldn't do this by turning back and focusing on the past.

He chose to not reflect on it anymore because he had a greater purpose. For Paul, living for Christ was worth far more than dwelling on the past. Despite my own history, I must choose to focus on running the race of faith well. I must give it all I've got and focus on Jesus, not my past.[3]

Lord, I know my past is ugly and filled with things I regret. It's filled with memories I wish I could undo. But, God, I'm choosing to no longer dwell on my past. I lay it all at your feet. Today, I choose to focus on you and the heavenly reward that awaits me. Holy Spirit, give me the strength that I need to depend on you every day as I run this race of faith.

DAY 17
KEEP ON

READ: PHILIPPIANS 4

"Keep putting into practice all you learned and received from me—everything you heard from me and saw me doing. Then the God of peace will be with you."

Philippians 4:9

"Information without implementation is useless."[1] Implementing God's truth into my life is vital. The Bible says that I should not just be a hearer of the Word but a doer.[2] This means I can't listen to a sermon and not make any changes to my life. I can't just read the Bible; I must *do* what it says!

Here, Paul encourages me to "*keep* putting into practice" all that I've learned and received. This is not just a one and done thing. I must take the teachings from the Bible and apply them day after day to my life. I must keep doing everything that I have learned and am continuing to learn. The most important step is to keep putting the Word into practice. I must be purposeful in it.

God, I want to keep putting what you show me into practice. This is where I have fallen short in the past: I stopped putting the teachings and revelations from your Word into my life. I practiced the ways of the world instead. Forgive me, Father! Cleanse my heart and transform my mind as I put your Word into practice even more every single day.

DAY 18
COMPLETE KNOWLEDGE

READ: COLOSSIANS 1

"We ask God to give you complete knowledge of his will and to give you spiritual wisdom and understanding. Then the way you live will always honor and please the Lord, and your lives will produce every kind of good fruit. All the while, you will grow as you learn to know God better and better."

Colossians 1:9–10

What is God's will? What are his desires and passions? The Apostle Paul prayed that I would know God's will and receive spiritual wisdom and understanding for my life. Having this results in a lifestyle that honors and pleases God—a life that will produce the good fruits of character and works. As this fruit grows, I will get to know God better and more intimately.

It all starts at the root: the "why." The motivations in my heart dictate my actions. The knowledge of God's will and desires properly direct my life. By having this knowledge, I will not only desire God's will for my life but his will for everything and everyone. The Lord wants people to be saved from their sins and mistakes, freed from their bondages and addictions, healed in their hearts and bodies, and transformed in their minds and lifestyles. Everything in my life should help these things become a reality for me and others. Therefore, I must live a lifestyle that lines up with the Bible's teachings. Living like this will honor and please God.

----◆----

Father, I ask for a full revelation of your will. Show me what concerns you most in this world. I want to live a life that is pleasing and honoring to you. Holy Spirit, give me the strength to choose holiness and righteousness in my life.

DAY 19
A CUTTING AWAY
READ: COLOSSIANS 2

"When you came to Christ, you were "circumcised," but not by a physical procedure. Christ performed a spiritual circumcision—the cutting away of your sinful nature... You were dead because of your sins and because your sinful nature was not yet cut away. Then God made you alive with Christ, for he forgave all our sins."

Colossians 2:11, 13

In Christ, my flesh, or sinful nature, was cut away when I gave my life to Christ. The inward desires and automatic pulls of sin were disarmed. Sin no longer has any power over me![1] I was dead in my sins, but now I am alive in Christ and set free from the power of sin. I am no longer under sin's tyranny. I don't have to do what my flesh urges me to do anymore. Now I have a choice on how to live.

If sin has lost its power, then why do I still struggle at times? The Bible tells me that I become the slave of whomever I choose to obey.[2] Jesus has become my new master, but now

I have the choice whether I will obey him. My choices in life show which master I want reigning over me. Do I choose to live under the old tyranny of sin and become enslaved again to a dead life? Or do I choose to obey God to live a life filled with freedom and righteousness?

———•◆•———

God, I'm so thankful that my old life has been cut away! You have rescued me from death and brought me into life. I am no longer bound to sin. Because sin has no power over me, I commit to living my life according to your Word. I refuse to line up with the old way of life. Living for you is my greatest desire.

DAY 20
MINDSET SHIFT
READ: COLOSSIANS 3

"Since you have been raised to new life with Christ, set your sights on the realities of heaven, where Christ sits in the place of honor at God's right hand... put to death the sinful, earthly things lurking within you. Have nothing to do with sexual immorality, impurity, lust, and evil desires... Put on your new nature, and be renewed as you learn to know your Creator and become like him."

Colossians 3:1, 5, 10

God has freed me from my sin, guilt, and shame. Now, my attitude must shift. I must change my mindset. I can't focus on this earthly kingdom anymore. Rather, I must continually focus on the Kingdom of God. I need to honor the new King and master I serve. This means I live my life in a manner showing I truly belong to Master Jesus and his Kingdom of Heaven.

Sexual immorality, impurity, lust, evil desires, anger, rage, malicious behavior, slander, and dirty language represent the old kingdom. I *must* kill off these behaviors and mindsets. I must throw them off like soiled clothes. Now I choose to practice kingdom behaviors: mercy, kindness, humility, gentleness, patience, forgiveness, and love. How do I make this mindset shift? By getting to know Christ and becoming like him. As I know Jesus more, his character will rub off on me, and my mind will be renewed. The only result is a transformed life.

Father, my desire is to set my sights on the realities of heaven. I want to focus on you. I ask that you keep renewing my mind. Help me shift my mindset to Kingdom behaviors and help me to quit acting like I live in the old kingdom. I want to represent you in this world. Transform my life, Holy Spirit!

DAY 21
LIVE WITH GRACE
READ: COLOSSIANS 4

"Live wisely among those who are not believers, and make the most of every opportunity. Let your conversation be gracious and attractive so that you will have the right response for everyone."

Colossians 4:5–6

H ow do I respond to those around me? It's intimidating when people ask questions about spiritual things. In these situations, there is a crippling pressure in wanting to answer correctly. Naturally, I think I need more knowledge, but it's not knowledge that I need. It's *grace*. People are always watching how I live. They want to see how I react to the pressures, stresses, and storms of life. They want to see how I act towards strangers, coworkers, family members, and friends.

When I live in a way that shows off God's love, grace, and power in my life—especially around those who don't believe—I will be attractive to others. People will be drawn to what I have, which is the truth of the Gospel. So, I should make the most of the opportunities I have and wisely share God's truth when it is appropriate. I must listen to the Holy Spirit's leading and guiding on what to do, what to say, and when to say it. If I do this, then I will have the right response to everyone.

God, help me live a life that is attracting other people to the Gospel and to a love relationship with you. Give me opportunities to share your love today. Help me be bold in sharing the truth, and provide the wisdom I need when people ask about my faith.

DAY 22
THE PROGRESSION

READ: 1 THESSALONIANS 1

"We know, dear brothers and sisters that God loves you and has chosen you to be his own people… So you received the message with joy from the Holy Spirit… you imitated both us and the Lord. As a result, you have become an example to all the believers… And now the word of the Lord is ringing out from you to people everywhere."

1 Thessalonians 1:4, 6–8

Paul showed a clear progression in my walk with the Lord. First, God pursued me. Because of his great love, he wanted me to be a part of his family.[1] God sent someone to share the Gospel with me, which I received with gladness. My life was forever changed when I surrendered my life to the Lordship of Jesus Christ.

The next step is shifting my mindset from living a selfish life to a God-centered life. How do I do that? What does it look like? The Apostle Paul said to look at the lives of people who are more mature in their faith and have walked with God longer than me. Success leaves clues. They are examples of how to live the God life. As I imitate their lives, my life begins to shine brighter for Christ to others around me.

———————◆————————

God, I want to be a light to everyone I encounter. Holy Spirit, show me how to be a living example of your grace and love to others. I ask for mature believers to be placed in my life so that I can emulate my life after theirs. Connect me with people who are passionate about you and live a holy life.

DAY 23
PLEASING GOD

READ: 1 THESSALONIANS 2

"For we speak as messengers approved by God to be entrusted with the Good News. Our purpose is to please God, not people. He alone examines the motives of our hearts."

1 Thessalonians 2:4

Who am I trying to please? Too often I am a people-pleaser. This isn't always a bad thing. I want my boss to be pleased with my work on the job. I want my future spouse to be pleased with me as we do life together. I want peace with my friends and family members, so I avoid conflict. The Apostle Paul essentially said, "Hey, we are boldly speaking about the Gospel whether people like it or receive it. We're not trying to get their approval. We're preaching because that is what God has called us to do."

When pleasing others starts to hinder me from doing what God has called *me* to do, then there is a problem. I can't let the opinions and opposition of other people hinder me from living my life completely for God. I can't let the ideologies of the culture influence my decisions. I can't even let the approval of close family or friends curtail the work of God in my life. No, I live to please God; therefore, I will follow his leading in every area of my life *no matter what!*

———————◆◆◆———————

God, I like pleasing those around me, but I want to please you more! It can be difficult to go against the grain of my friends' or family's opinions, but if I'm walking with you, nothing else matters. Holy Spirit, give me the strength to be bold for you. You know what is best for me, so I choose to follow your leading everywhere. When a tough situation arises or a tough decision needs to be made, give me the wisdom I need. I surrender my life to you.

DAY 24
GOD'S WILL AND CALLING
READ: 1 THESSALONIANS 3:1-4:12

"God's will is for you to be holy, so stay away from all sexual sin... God has called us to live holy lives, not impure lives. Therefore, anyone who refuses to live by these rules is not disobeying human teaching but is rejecting God, who gives his Holy Spirit to you."

1 Thessalonians 4:3, 7–8

What is God's will for my life? What am I called to do? What is my life's purpose? What is it God wants me to do? I have asked these questions often and in so many ways. God expresses his will and calling clearly for me in this passage.

God's will for every believer is to be holy. This means God's will for me is to live a pure life separated from the world. I can know I am fulfilling God's will and calling when I am staying away from *all* sexual sin. All of it. Oh, how I failed to do this for so long! But now I'm free! I can clearly hear from God because I am choosing to live a pure and holy life.

Choosing to stay away from sexual sin grants me control over my life so I can live in holiness and honor.[1] Sexual sin causes me to be out of control; I become a slave to sins, fleshly desires, and addictions.[2] I become compelled to fulfill the lusts of my flesh. The freedom to live away from these things comes from the control that is developed through abstinence. As I stay away from sexual sin, I will learn how to control my body and develop self-control.

———————————

God, I want to do your will. I want to fulfill the calling you have on my life. Therefore, I choose to stay away from all sexual sin. Forgive me for when I have not done this. Sexual sin corrupts and destroys, but I want to be holy and live with honor. Teach me, Holy Spirit, how to control my mind, body, and emotions as I stay clear of these sins. Show me how to live the life you have called me to live.

DAY 25
THE RETURN

READ: 1 THESSALONIANS 4:13-5:11

"For God chose to save us through our Lord Jesus Christ, not to pour out his anger on us. Christ died for us so that, whether we are dead or alive when he returns, we can live with him forever."

1 Thessalonians 5:9-10

There is great encouragement when I focus on the Lord's return. The Apostle Paul encourages me with the promise of the rapture of the church.[1] In just a twinkling of an eye, all the other believers on earth and I will be caught up into the clouds. Our earthly bodies will be transformed into new heavenly bodies.[2] I will get to meet all the believers, dead and alive, in the clouds with Jesus! This means there will be a reunion with my family and friends who were believers in Christ and have already died. I will get to see them again. I will be reunited with my loved ones and with Christ for eternity.

Jesus Christ is returning soon. He is going to establish his Kingdom here on earth.[3] His return is going to come unexpectantly, like a thief in the night, so I must be ready for his return.[4] When he does come, I will experience life like never before!

———————◆•◆•◆———————

Father, thank you for this encouraging word. I don't have to grieve like those who have no hope for my hope is in you. I will get to see my loved ones again, and I get to be in your presence for eternity. Help me to be alert and clearheaded.[5] I want to be sober minded as I look forward to your return. Come quickly, Lord Jesus!

DAY 26
HONORABLE LIVING

READ: 2 THESSALONIANS 1-2

"So we keep on praying for you, asking our God to enable you to live a life worthy of his call. May he give you the power to accomplish all the good things your faith prompts you to do. Then the name of our Lord Jesus will be honored because of the way you live, and you will be honored along with him. This is all made possible because of the grace of our God and Lord, Jesus Christ."

2 Thessalonians 1:11–12

The Apostle Paul had a twofold prayer. First, he prayed for God to give me the power to live a worthy life of the Gospel. I'm reminded that God will provide the power that I need to do what he asks. To build my faith, I must rely on God's strength. I can't depend on my own strength, for apart from Christ, I can do nothing.[1] But in him nothing is impossible![2] God will give me the power and the will to do what pleases him.[3]

Paul also prayed that my life would honor Christ. Living a worthy life results in a double honor. First, God is honored by how I live. His name and reputation are well represented to the world. Jesus is praised for the great things that get accomplished because they will seem impossible to the world. Secondly, I get the honor of being associated with Christ! I get recognized as someone who lives an honorable life—a life of integrity. What an incredible honor to be acknowledged as an ambassador of Christ!

God, thank you for choosing me to represent you to a dying world. I am not worthy, yet you changed my life so that I could be a part of your mission. I want to do what you say, so help me fulfill everything you have called me to do. Holy Spirit, empower me today. I choose to rely on your strength so that you will get all the glory.

DAY 27
IDLE LIVES

READ: 2 THESSALONIANS 3

"And now, dear brothers and sisters, we give you this command in the name of our Lord Jesus Christ: Stay away from all believers who live idle lives and don't follow the tradition they received from us."

2 Thessalonians 3:6

Who I surround myself with affects how I live. It has been said that I will become like the five people closest to me. People have an influence over my life, whether I admit or realize it. Paul warned the church in Corinth that "bad company corrupts good character."[1] There are people who are not living a godly lifestyle, and their influence doesn't help me live a life that honors God. These people are idle in their faith and everyday living. Their laziness can encourage and influence me to be idle and lazy as well. I must stay away from people like this!

There are also people who claim to be Christians but aren't living like it. Their lifestyles are walking contradictions to their beliefs. The antidote for their potentially poisonous influence in my life is to stay away from them. Therefore, I must instead surround myself with like-minded believers who will encourage me to stand strong in my faith and pursue God with everything that I have.

———————◆•◆•◆———————

Lord, there are many people in this world who live idle lives. Many aren't living according to what you have declared in your Word. Help me to avoid these people's influence. Holy Spirit, I ask for on-fire Christians to come into my life who will encourage me to live for you! Let their influence motivate me to stir others up in their faith. Use me to be the positive, Christian influence in someone else's life.

DAY 28
CONTRADICTIONS

READ: 1 TIMOTHY 1

"For the law was not intended for people who do what is right... The law is for people who are sexually immoral, or who practice homosexuality, or are slave traders, liars, promise breakers, or who do anything else that contradicts the wholesome teaching that comes from the glorious Good News entrusted to me by our blessed God."

1 Timothy 1:9–11

How I live is the proof of my faith. How I behave is how I believe. PMO falls into the "sexually immoral" category in this passage. Because I was involved with PMO, I was living in sexual immorality. This lifestyle contradicts the truth of the Gospel. It contradicts God's will to be holy and calling to live a holy life. The law was written to show me that these lifestyle choices are wrong, and verses like these pronounce me guilty of breaking those laws. The Gospel is that Jesus paid my death penalty for me so that I can now live a free life away from sexual immorality (PMO) by accepting him as Lord and receiving his gift of grace, forgiveness, and mercy by faith.

With that in mind, here is Paul's exhortation and admonishment: "Cling to your faith in Christ, and keep your conscience clear. For some people have deliberately violated their consciences; as a result, their faith has been shipwrecked."[1]

Father, help me hold on to you. I want to continually keep my heart clear before you. I will not choose sin, and I will not violate my conscience. I refuse to let it become seared. I want my heart to be soft and tender before you. I will not risk shipwrecking my faith. You are worth too much!

DAY 29
LEADERSHIP

READ: 1 TIMOTHY 3

"This is a trustworthy saying: 'If someone aspires to be a church leader, he desires an honorable position.'"

1 Timothy 3:1

Church leadership is an important thing. It's not for everyone, and there are certain standards on how leaders in the church should live. As a young pastor, Timothy needed guidance on how to select high-quality leaders for his church. Paul gave Timothy several qualifications: A leader is to be the husband of one wife (or a one-wife man)[1] and manage his household well.[2] He must have a good reputation in and outside of the church.[3] A leader should be hospitable and able to teach[4] and not be new in the faith.[5] He shouldn't be given to alcohol or a lover of money, and he should be gentle, not violent or quarrelsome.[6]

These are high qualifications that should be closely observed before placing someone into a leadership role in the church. But how do I test in these categories? If I am going to be a leader in the church, how well do I perform in these areas?

Do I manage my household well? Am I gentle? Do I have a good reputation of living with integrity? I must examine myself honestly. If I am falling short in an area, I need to make the appropriate adjustments in my life to change for the better.

———————◆•◆•◆———————

Father, I want to make sure I live an honorable life. I don't want to fall into the devil's trap due to immaturity or pride. Lord, help me live appropriately! I want to be used by you. I want to become the leader you have called me to be, so fortify the areas where I am doing well. Holy Spirit, grow me in the areas where I am lacking. I can't do this without you.

DAY 30
GODLY TRAINING
READ: 1 TIMOTHY 4

"Physical training is good, but training for godliness is much better, promising benefits in this life and in the life to come."
Timothy 4:7

I really enjoy the gym. Training my physical body hasn't always been a pleasurable experience, but I love seeing the results that come from putting in the hard work. I enjoy feeling stronger and more confident in what I can do. I like the challenge of pushing myself to run harder, lift heavier, or move more effectively.

Paul encouraged Timothy, his son in the faith, to focus *more* on training for godliness. Physical training helps me now, but my body is aging and will eventually die. Training in godliness not only helps me today but also equips me for eternity in heaven. Therefore, while it is very important for me to take care of my physical body, it's far more important to pour energy into training my spirit.

———◆•◆•◆———

God, thank you for this reminder today. Yes, I need to take care of my body; it's a temple of the Holy Spirit.¹ But I don't want to neglect taking care of my spirit and my faith either. Help me grow stronger. Show me how to increase my faith and to develop a deeper relationship with you. Show me how to become more like Jesus. Just like I have committed to physical training in the gym, God, I commit to training in godliness through prayer, reading your Word, and intimate times of worship.

DAY 31
PAUL'S CHARGE

READ: 1 TIMOTHY 6

"But you, Timothy, are a man of God; so run from all these evil things. Pursue righteousness and a godly life, along with faith, love, perseverance, and gentleness. Fight the good fight for the true faith. Hold tightly to the eternal life to which God has called you, which you have declared so well before many witnesses."
1 Timothy 6:11-12

Timothy was a young pastor in a sexually immoral and corrupt city filled with temple prostitution, idol worship, and false teachers trying to infiltrate the Christian church. Paul charged Timothy to run from the evil practices around him! Run from sexual immorality. Run from the love of money and pointless arguments. Don't chase after these things. Instead, pursue righteousness, holy living, and the eternal truth of Jesus Christ.

Society today greatly resembles Ephesus. I am surrounded by overly sexualized media in movies, TV, social media, and music. There is an ever-growing pressure from the culture to embrace sexual promiscuity and perversion. My response is to be the same as Timothy's: Run! Flee from the evil and sexual practices that surround me. I can't crumble under the pressures to conform to the patterns of this world. No, I must choose to have my mind transformed by renewing my mind.[1] I must pursue righteousness and the things that please God.

———————◆•◆•◆———————

God, I will pursue righteousness and a godly life. I will pursue a life of faith, perseverance, and gentleness. I will continue to fight and hold tightly to the truth. Real life is all about you, Jesus! I commit my entire life to you and your service!

DAY 32
PURE FOR A PURPOSE

READ: 2 TIMOTHY 1-2

"For God saved us and called us to live a holy life... If you keep yourself pure, you will be a special utensil for honorable use. Your life will be clean, and you will be ready for the Master to use you for every good work. Run from anything that stimulates youthful lusts. Instead, pursue righteous living, faithfulness, love, and peace."

2 Timothy 1:9, 2:21-22

One of the signs of a maturing faith is the desire to please God through service. As I grow in my faith, my desire shifts from wanting my needs to be met to wanting to help meet the needs of others. This transforms into a desire for a deeper calling: to be used by God for a special purpose. Paul illustrates this calling with household utensils. In his day, there were gold and silver utensils and wood and clay utensils. Today, it would be the difference between paper plates and fine China plates. The paper plates are used for ordinary meals, but the fine China comes out for the special occasions!

I want to be a gold or silver utensil. I want to be a fine China plate that God can use for special occasions. Ordinary use is nice, but I want to be used in a special way for the Kingdom of God. Therefore, I will run from anything that will stimulate old lusts of the flesh. I will pursue righteousness, faithfulness, and peaceful living.

God, thank you for the calling to live a holy life. Not only do you do this to protect me, but you do it to give me a greater purpose in life. You have called me to be a tool for honorable use, so I will run from anything that used to trip me up. I refuse to pursue the ways of the old life. Instead, with your help, Holy Spirit, I will pursue the things that please you: righteous living, love, and peace. I want to be used by you. Give me the grace and strength to live a holy life.

DAY 33
REMAIN FAITHFUL

READ: 2 TIMOTHY 3

"You should know this, Timothy, that in the
last days there will be very difficult times."
2 Timothy 3:1

It's easy to see that this description of the last days applies to *today*. I am living in the age where this is a reality. There are many people who are rejecting God to pursue their own pleasures. There are many Christians who have been deceived into believing the lies of the world and transient opinions of culture. Other Christians know what the Bible declares as true and righteous, yet they compromise their integrity and morals for pleasures that will never satisfy their souls. Some Christians have been hurt, disappointed, and abused (physically and emotionally) into a state of mind where they have decided to deconstruct their faith and walk away from God.

These are the days in which I live. This is the age that the Lord has placed me. I was born for a time such as this. Paul encouraged Timothy, and me as well, with these words: "But you must remain faithful to the things you have been taught."[1] "Preach the word of God."[2]

God, I will stay faithful to your Word. I will preach the Word. I will teach the Word, and I will obey the Word. No matter how hard life may be, I won't give up. I will stay true. I refuse to let the difficult times around me sway me into living a life contrary to the life you have called me to live. Holy Spirit, give me the wisdom I need to navigate these extreme days.

DAY 34
HOW TO LIVE
READ: TITUS 1

"I have been sent to proclaim faith to those
God has chosen and to teach them to know the
truth that shows them how to live godly lives."
Titus 1:1

The Bible is the manual on life and Godliness. It shows me that God has given me everything I need to live a godly life.[1] The Word declares how God has supernaturally empowered me by the Holy Spirit to live a righteous and holy life. The Bible teaches me that the same resurrection power that raised Jesus from the dead now enables me to live out a godly life, and now I have been given the desire and power to do what pleases him.[2]

In this passage, the Apostle Paul highlighted an important facet of living a godly life: knowing the truth of God. I have the desire (motive) to live godly, and I have the power (ability) to live godly. Now, I must obtain the knowledge of the truth to walk godly (action).

God's Word doesn't just give me information; it gives me application. The truths in the Bible shouldn't stay in my head.

They are meant to drop down into my heart and become convictions. To live a godly life, I must apply the things I am taught. Jesus said that "If you abide in My word [hold fast to My teachings and live in accordance with them], you are truly My disciples. And you will know the Truth, and the Truth will set you free."[3] Everything changes once I apply the Word of God to my life!

———————◆•◆•◆———————

Father, I thank you for your Word. Thank you for showing me how to live a godly life. Thank you for giving me the steps I need to take to be free forever. Holy Spirit, I ask for you to continually reveal truth to me. I want to grow deeper with you.

DAY 35
BEFORE AND AFTER

READ: TITUS 3

*"Once we, too, were foolish and disobedient.
We were misled and became slaves to many
lusts and pleasures. Our lives were full of evil
and envy, and we hated each other. But—
When God our Savior revealed his kindness
and love, he saved us, not because of the righteous things we had done, but because of his
mercy. He washed away our sins, giving us a
new birth and new life through the Holy Spirit.
He generously poured out the Spirit upon us
through Jesus Christ our Savior. Because of his
grace he made us right in his sight and gave
us confidence that we will inherit eternal life."*

Titus 3:3–7

The grace of God is truly amazing. I once was foolish
and led by anger, lust, PMO, and insecurities. I was
enslaved to my past and my fleshly desires. My life was filled
with all kinds of evil, but God showed me his loving kindness.
He saved me because of his mercy and love. God has declared

me righteous before him![1] I have been given a fresh start, a new life through the Holy Spirit![2] I have been made right in his sight because of his grace!

———————◆•◆•◆———————

Father, I am overwhelmed and in awe of the grace you have poured into my life. I didn't deserve any of your kindness. I didn't deserve any of your mercy, yet you offered it to me gladly. It gave you great joy to bring me into your family.[3] Thank you for your amazing grace! Thank you for the confidence of eternal life. I surrender my life to you, Lord Jesus. Use me to further your Kingdom.

DAY 36
A LITTLE WHILE

READ: PHILEMON 1

*"It seems you lost Onesimus for a little while
so that you could have him back forever."*
Philemon 1:15

O nesimus, a slave, ran away from his master Philemon. Paul met Onesimus and shared Christ with him. As a result, Onesimus became a Christian and Paul sent him back to Philemon with this letter. Paul wrote that Philemon lost Onesimus for a little while to have him back forever. Their relationship wouldn't look the same. It would be better and deeper because they are now brothers in the Lord.

I can't help but think of all the people I know who have walked away from God to pursue passions that can never be satisfied. Just like the prodigal's son, they have run away from their Father's house to live their own way.[1] They know what is right, but they have become deceived in their disobedience. These people, like Onesimus, have become lost. But I know that in a little while, I will have them back forever. They *will* return home!

———◆•◆•◆———

God, there are people I love and care about who have walked away from you. I ask for you to cut off this season of sin in their lives. Let there be a fence of thornbushes around them so anything they do apart from you would fail and be unfulfilling.[2] Do what it takes to bring them back to you! Remove the blinders from their eyes to see and soften their hearts to hear the truth.[3] They may be lost, but they will come back to be with me forever!

DAY 37
THE DANGERS OF UNBELIEF
READ: HEBREWS 3:1-4:12

"Be careful then, dear brothers and sisters.
Make sure that your own hearts are not evil
and unbelieving, turning you away from the
living God. You must warn each other every
day, while it is still 'today,' so that none of you
will be deceived by sin and hardened against
God."

Hebrews 3:12–13

My heart must be pure and trusting before God to enter the promised rest and share in all that belongs to Christ. The Israelites were not able to enter the promised rest due to their unbelief.[1] This unbelief demonstrated itself through their *rebellion* and *disobedience. Rebellion* is the attitude of the heart;[2] *disobedience* is the action from that attitude.[3]

The writer of Hebrews described a *willful* action against what God has said. To have an attitude of wanting to do something contrary to God's word is rebellion. The Israelite's hearts were hardened by their disobedience, and they did not enter

God's rest. Their actions and attitudes were linked to their *unbelief.* "Only we who *believe* can enter his rest."[4]

God, I want to have faith, not unbelief. I want to live in your rest now and enter eternal rest later. Forgive me for my rebellious heart where I have desired to do things contrary to your Word. I will not harden my heart any longer by my disobedience. I choose to live my life in complete obedience to you. I trust you with my life, Lord Jesus!

DAY 38
HE KNOWS

READ: HEBREWS 4:13-16

"This High Priest of ours understands our weaknesses, for he faced all of the same testings we do, yet he did not sin. So let us come boldly to the throne of our gracious God. There we will receive his mercy, and we will find grace to help us when we need it most."

Hebrews 4:15-16

No matter what trial, temptation, or testing that I go through, Jesus understands. No matter what emotions I feel or pain that I endure, Jesus understands. He was faced with all the same testings during his life on earth and did not sin. In his humanity, Jesus relied on the power of the Holy Spirit to show me that it can be done. He is the example to me of one who lived a holy life fully dependent on the Holy Spirit.

Jesus knows and understands what I'm going through because he experienced it too! So, when I am tempted, angry, lonely, or sad, I can come to God. I can come to him when life is overwhelming or peaceful. No matter what I need, I can come boldly into the throne room of God to receive all the grace and power that I need to endure. He knows, and he understands.

God, it is amazing that you understand what I am going through. You understand my weaknesses and temptations. You were able to live a life dependent on the Holy Spirit to avoid temptations and make it through trials. So, God, I came boldly into your throne room today to receive grace to make it through. I need your grace to avoid and resist temptations. I need your grace to comfort and heal my emotions. I need your grace to get through this storm in my life. I need you desperately. I surrender everything to you, Lord Jesus. Take all of me!

DAY 39
GOD'S WILL
READ: HEBREWS 10:1-18

"For God's will was for us to be made holy by the sacrifice of the body of Jesus Christ, once for all time."

Hebrews 10:10

It is God's purpose for me to become holy by Jesus' sacrifice. His will is for my sins to be forgiven. It is God's desire that I be saved and understand the truth.[1] God's ultimate purpose is for mankind to be reconciled back to him through the once-and-for-all sacrifice of his son, Jesus Christ.

Holiness deals with purity and separation. God wants people to be cleansed from their sins. He wants his bride, the Church, to be without spot or wrinkle.[2] The sacrifice Jesus made—his spilled blood—forgave my sins and washed them away forever. It is God's will for me to be purified by that blood and live a pure life. It is also God's will for me to be separated from my sin, the world, and death so that I may be exclusively his. God wants all of me, even the ugly parts: rebellion, sin, addiction, disappointment, hopelessness, sadness, anger, depression, and everything in between.

God, I give you all of me. I give you the good, the bad, and the ugly parts of my life. Take it all. Make me holy. I have received your life by receiving forgiveness for my sins through Jesus' sacrifice. Now, Holy Spirit, do your will in my heart, mind, and soul. I give you everything.

DAY 40

I WILL!

READ: HEBREWS 10:19-39

"So do not throw away this confident trust in the Lord. Remember the great reward it brings you! Patient endurance is what you need now, so that you will continue to do God's will."
Hebrews 10:35–36

The journey of faith can be tiresome. During a 26.2-mile race, marathon runners can become tired and get tempted to give up before reaching the finish line. But the runner doesn't quit. The athlete keeps moving forward to complete the race. There will be days when my race of faith will be difficult, and I will be tempted to quit or sit idly on the sidelines. The encouragement from the writer of Hebrews is to patiently endure! Be faithful! I can't give up and throw away my trust in God and his promises because there is a reward if I persevere: an abundant life now and for eternity.

God has called me to live a holy life. I didn't used to live a completely pure life, and it hindered me from living to my maximum potential. How could I receive all that God had promised me while pursuing lusts and PMO? Why would God give me more responsibilities when I hadn't been faithful with what I already had?

Now that I have freedom in Christ, I will fully pursue a life of integrity so I can receive all that God has for my life. I will fulfill God's will to stay away from sexual sin[1] so I can be a golden utensil to be used for a special purpose.[2]

———————•◆•———————

Father, I remember when I first learned about Jesus and how excited I was to be devoted and faithful to you. Along the way, I have become weary and wanted to give up. But I set my eyes on you, Jesus. I don't want to throw away my trust in you or become weary anymore. The decision has been made today: I will not give up. I will be faithful. I will persevere to the end.

DAY 41
BY FAITH

READ: HEBREWS 11

"Faith shows the reality of what we hope for;
it is the evidence of things we cannot see."
Hebrews 11:1

aith. It is the cornerstone aspect of the Christian life. Everything is rooted in it. Everything that I live and trust in is based upon faith. The writer of Hebrews listed multiple examples of people who lived their lives in faith and what that looked like for each of them. They all *demonstrated* their faith in their lives. Abel demonstrated his faith through obedience. Enoch demonstrated his faith by walking continually in fellowship with God. Abraham and Sarah demonstrated their faith by patiently waiting for a promise. Noah demonstrated his faith by being prudent about future events.

My life *must* be rooted in faith. Faith is knowing that I have received a promise, even when I don't possess it. Even when I don't see it, I still trust in God.

———◆·◆·◆———

Father, I commit to living my life fully in faith. I choose to remember the promises you have given me personally in prayer and in your Word. Though I may not yet possess them, I still believe I will receive them. I will see restoration in the broken relationships around me. I will see my mind renewed. I will be completely free of addictions. My testimony will encourage and influence other people's lives. Thank you, Lord God, for your promises. I will remain faithful to you.

DAY 42
A SECOND WIND
READ: HEBREWS 12

"So take a new grip with your tired hands and strengthen your weak knees. Mark out a straight path for your feet so that those who are weak and lame will not fall but become strong."

Hebrews 12:12–13

After recalling the heroes of the faith,[1] the author of Hebrews wrote a three-step strategy that will reenergize me when I am feeling weak and tired in my race of faith. First, I must remove any hindrances in my life that may slow me down or cause me to trip, especially those sins that usually make me fall.[2] Next, I must refocus my gaze and keep it on Jesus.[3] Looking to the right or to the left will cause me to veer off course or step off the path. By fixing my eyes on Jesus, I can remain focused on what is most important. Third, I must remember what Jesus endured: public hostility, shame, rejection, pain, and crucifixion. Jesus was able to endure to the end by focusing on the great joy ahead of having a restored relationship with humanity by paying the price for its rebellion and sin. He did not give up even though he asked another way.[4]

With this strategy implemented, I have the motivation and second wind to keep running. My grip on my faith and God becomes tighter. My knees become strong again, so now I can run a little harder. And by choosing to endure through the tough times, my example will have a profound effect on others. By moving forward, I will clear paths and leave clues for others to become strong too.

———•:◆:•———

Lord Jesus, I choose to fix my eyes only on you! I remember the sacrifice you made for me. Today, I mark out a clear path of faith for me, and I choose to run with all that I've got. I believe my journey can and will help others that are weak to be strong in their faith!

DAY 43
NOT ABANDONED

READ: HEBREWS 13

"For God has said, "I will never fail you. I will never abandon you."

Hebrews 13:5

R ejection is a hard thing to experience. It's something everyone encounters at some point. I experienced rejection early in life from my mother. Then, over the years, I was rejected by friends, girls, peers, and other family members. The cruel effect of rejection is that it made me feel abandoned. It made me feel as if nobody cared about or wanted me. Rejection left a wound that took root into my heart, and with every encounter with it, this root dug deeper and deeper. It eventually grew so deep that it changed my outlook on how people responded to me. It changed my expectations in life. I believed people thought the worst about me. I expected the bleakest results in my relationships.

This all changed when I found freedom in Christ! Jesus declared that he has never abandoned me or failed me. And he never will. He has always been there, even when I didn't perceive him. He has always protected me, even when I thought he was absent.

———————•◦•◆•◦•———————

God, I am accepted by you. I am adopted into your family.[1] I have a family who loves and cares about me. I have a church family that I can turn to when I am in trouble and need. I have friends who have my back no matter what. I get my acceptance from you, Lord Jesus, and from these people that I love. I get the love I want and need from you and them. Thank you, Father, for promising that you will never fail me and that you will never abandon me. Through the highs and lows in my life, you always have and will always be there for me.

DAY 44
SO THAT

READ: 1 PETER 1

"So you must live as God's obedient children. Don't slip back into your old ways of living to satisfy your own desires. You didn't know any better then. But now you must be holy in everything you do, just as God who chose you is holy."

1 Peter 1:14–15

There is a priceless inheritance waiting for me in heaven.[1] I should be filled with joy because of this promise, even when I go through difficult trials in life. Considering this eternal reward awaiting on the other side of earthly trials, Peter detailed a challenge to me to live differently: Because of the eternal salvation given to me, I must prepare my mind and exercise self-control.[2] Christ is returning with eternal salvation, so I can't slip back into old living. Instead, I must live a holy life.[3] God doesn't show favoritism and will judge me according to my actions, so I must live in the fear of the Lord while here on earth.[4] Since God cleansed me from all my sins, I must show deep love for other Christians with a pure heart.[5]

Because the Gospel was preached to me and I have been born again, I must get rid of evil behavior.[6]

———————————————

Father, thank you for the eternal salvation you have provided for me by sending Jesus to die for my sins. Help me to walk out all these challenges every day. Even when trials and temptations come, help me endure so my faith in you will be strengthened. Equip me to live in the fear of the Lord so that I will not slip back into the old way of living.

DAY 45
KEEP AWAY

READ: 1 PETER 2

"Dear friends, I warn you as 'temporary residents and foreigners' to keep away from worldly desires that wage war against your very souls... For you are free, yet you are God's slaves, so don't use your freedom as an excuse to do evil."

1 Peter 2:11, 16

The Bible is filled with calls to righteous living and here is no exception. Peter began this chapter with the identity of the Christian. I am not the person I used to be. I have been pulled out of the darkness and have been identified as a member of God's royal priesthood. I am no longer a nobody; I am God's own possession. I belong to God now. Because my identity has changed, I must live accordingly. I must keep away from worldly desires that are associated with the old life. I can't go back and live the way I used to live. I must now live an honorable life in public and in private. I am called to be a man of integrity. Therefore, I should live in such a way that if someone were to accuse me of something evil, no one would believe it!

I can't abuse my freedom either. Just because I am free does not mean that I can cheapen the grace of God or treat sin lightly. No, I choose to live a holy life. I choose to hate the things that God hates and love the things that he loves. I used to be enslaved to sin and had to answer its beckoning call. Now, I am free to choose, so I choose righteousness, godliness, and love over the evil desires of this world that only lead to death.

------◆•◆•◆------

Father, I proclaim that I will use my freedom to glorify you! I want to live my life to honor you in all I do. I will not slip back into the old ways of life, but I will choose to keep away from those things so I can pursue you with all my strength.

DAY 46
SUFFER FOR CHRIST
READ: 1 PETER 4

"So then, since Christ suffered physical pain, you must arm yourselves with the same attitude he had, and be ready to suffer, too. For if you have suffered physically for Christ, you have finished with sin. You won't spend the rest of your lives chasing your own desires, but you will be anxious to do the will of God."

1 Peter 4:1–2

Suffering isn't a popular subject, but it is an area that must be expected for every true follower of Christ. Jesus said that I will experience trials,[1] be hated by men,[2] and face persecution.[3] This will happen because it happened to him,[4] and Jesus was perfect—without any sin! When I do face ridicule, suffering, persecution, or a trial, I can consider it pure joy![5] It will mean I have "leveled up" in my walk with Christ. I will have been deemed worthy to face this persecution and honorably share the name of my Lord.[6]

Suffering for Christ also puts another nail in the coffin of my fleshly desires. I will no longer desire to fulfill selfish passions, lusts, or PMO. Instead, my passion will grow stronger to do the will of God. I will draw closer to the Holy Spirit for strength, comfort, and guidance. As I continue to seek God for his grace during troubling times, the greater I will desire his will alone.

———————•◆•———————

God, I don't know when I will face persecution, but I trust in you. You are worth everything to me, so a short-lived trial is nothing in comparison to the glory of my reward in heaven. Eternity with you is worth any moment of temporary pain on earth. Holy Spirit, equip me with the same attitude of Christ so that I too can patiently endure anything that comes my way.

DAY 47
DO THESE THINGS

READ: 2 PETER 1

"By his divine power, God has given us everything we need for living a godly life... So, dear brothers and sisters, work hard to prove that you really are among those God has called and chosen. Do these things, and you will never fall away."

2 Peter 1:3, 10

The Holy Spirit has given me everything I need to live a holy and righteous life. He has empowered me to do it. Therefore, I am going to work to showcase the power of God through my changed life. God has called and chosen me to be in a relationship with him and to be an ambassador of Christ to this world.[1]

If I am going to showcase this grace in my life to the world, then I must develop spiritual maturity. Peter explained a growth progression that begins with having a heart change (moral excellence). It then progresses into knowledge, self-control, patient endurance, godliness, love for other Christians, and then love for everyone. Too many people try to grow in other areas without having the foundation of the previous area. What's the result? They become shortsighted or blind and forget "that God delivered [them] from the old life of sin so that now [they] can live a strong, good life for the Lord."[2] The good news is that if I choose to develop myself the right way, then I will never fall away. I will have the firm foundation of Christ established in my life, and nothing will be able to shake my faith.[3]

—————◆•◆•◆—————

God, thank you for giving me everything I need to live a godly life. I want my life to showcase your glory to others. Let my life be a testimony of the wonderful changes you have made within me. Holy Spirit, empower me to do the right things to grow strong and mature in my faith. Help me build a strong foundation in you, so that when troubles, trials, or temptations come my way, I will be able to stand firm and never fall away.

DAY 48
FALSE TEACHERS
READ: 2 PETER 2-3

*"There were also false prophets in Israel, just
as there will be false teachers among you. They
will cleverly teach destructive heresies and
even deny the Master who bought them."*
                                        2 Peter 2:1

The world is filled with all sorts of evil. False teachers of
the Gospel propagate their evil with the façade of true
Christianity. Their "clever teachings" err from the truth of
God's word and lead people astray just to take their money.[1]
There are teachers who proudly flaunt their immoral living
and lure hurting and vulnerable people right back into the sin
they have barely escaped from.[2] They promise freedom, but
their methods only lead people back into bondage.[3]

Peter's descriptions exemplify today's culture perfectly. This
is a sign to me that Jesus' return to earth is closer than ever
before. Even with all this evil in the world, God chooses to be
patient so that more people can be saved and spared from his
coming judgment. God doesn't want anyone to be destroyed,
but his desire is for *everyone* to repent![4]

Lord, there are many false teachers around me that are preaching a false Gospel, deceiving people into greed and immorality, and diminishing the authority of what you have said is right and holy in your Word. I ask, Holy Spirit, for you to fill me with supernatural wisdom to be able to discern between the truth and the lies in society. Protect my mind from deceiving thoughts and teachings that could hinder my walk with you. Thank you, Lord Jesus, that you are not being slow but patient so that many can repent and be saved. I pray that many will turn from their wicked ways and embrace a love relationship with you.

DAY 49
YOU CAN BE SURE
READ: 1 JOHN 1-2

"And we can be sure that we know him if we obey his commandments... those who obey God's word truly show how completely they love him."

1 John 2:3, 5

Jesus said to John many years before, "Those who accept my commandments and obey them are the ones who love me... All who love me will do what I say."[1] Obedience to God's word is one of several proofs that help me know if someone is living in the light and truly knows God. These are tests to see whether someone really is a Christian.

The biggest litmus test to see where someone is in his or her relationship with God is if he or she is obedient to God's Word. If I love Jesus, then my response will be a desire to obey what he says. It won't be a burden because obedience will come out of a loving desire to please him rather than a duty to fulfill. I don't want to be a self-deceived liar because I have not obeyed God's Word.[2] I was lying to myself when I was stuck in PMO—I wasn't obeying the words of Christ! There was something off in my love relationship with God that needed restoration. Now I live in God's light of freedom, and it is truly a delight to obey God's Word! What a joy it is to desire God fully with a pure heart!

———•◆•———

God, thank you for showing me that my love for you is not partial anymore but complete. I'm sorry I grew cold in my relationship with you, but now I am fueled with a burning desire to know you more intimately. I want to experience you in a deeper and greater way. My desire is to obey you, not out of duty, but out of a deep love for you. Holy Spirit, draw me closer to you!

DAY 50
LIVING AND LOVING

READ: 1 JOHN 3

"This is how we know who the children of God are and who the children of the devil are: Anyone who does not do what is right is not God's child, nor is anyone who does not love their brother and sister."

1 John 3:10

There is a deep connection between living in fellowship with God and loving others—especially fellow Christians. Living in fellowship with God means that I am obeying his commandments[1] and not making a habit of sinning.[2] An addictive cycle like PMO is painful to put against verses like these. The Scriptures revealed that something in my life was not right, and I needed God to intervene. Since God called me to be obedient, then, with the Holy Spirit's help, I must live a holy life.

Living in fellowship with God also means that I am loving, serving, and helping other Christians. Those who don't love others don't truly have God's love in them.[3] I want to demonstrate that my faith is real through my actions, not just words.[4]

Jesus demonstrated his love for me by giving up his life for mine. Since he did this for me, my only response is to be obedient and to extend that same love to others.

———————◆•◆•◆———————

Thank you, Jesus, for giving up your life for me. Your sacrifice didn't just bring me from death to life; it gave me an example of how to love others deeply, fully, and sacrificially. Help me show compassion and love to others—especially those who are believers. Let the transformation of my heart extend into my actions. Holy Spirit, show me ways I can serve and encourage the Christians around me.

DAY 51
FIGHT FROM VICTORY
READ: 1 JOHN 4

"But you belong to God, my dear children. You have already won a victory over those people, because the Spirit who lives in you is greater than the spirit who lives in the world."

1 John 4:4

The first part of this verse is very powerful for two reasons. First, it gives me my *position*. By believing in Jesus Christ, I am now a child of God.[1] I have been adopted into his family.[2] I'm now considered his and part of his kingdom.[3]

Secondly, it gives me a *proclamation*. I have already won the battle because Jesus has already won the war! He did this when he put Satan to public shame when he rose from the dead.[4] Death thought it had won at the cross, but there was victory over it at the resurrection of Christ. Therefore, I don't fight my battles *for* victory; I fight *from* victory. I fight and endure life's skirmishes knowing the result of the war. I have won because Jesus has already won. Now I occupy earth until Jesus returns to rule from Jerusalem.[5]

The final part of this verse gives me a *principle*. God is stronger. Period. The Holy Spirit living in me is far more powerful than Satan, the god of this earth.[6] So when I face trials and battles in my life, I can stand firm on the truth that the Holy Spirit will empower me to endure. He is greater than any other spiritual being in the heavenly realm. Jesus has overcome the world![7]

———————◆•◆•◆———————

God, I am so grateful that you won the war! Help me to remember my position in your family—a child of God. Use me to proclaim the victory that is found in you. Holy Spirit, continually remind me that you empower me. You are greater than any evil or spirit that is of this world. You are greater than any temptation or trial that may come against or upon me. I have nothing to fear in this life because you are with me. I am strong and confident because of you.

DAY 52
HE HEARS, HE GIVES

READ: 1 JOHN 5

"And we are confident that he hears us when-
ever we ask for anything that pleases him. And
since we know he hears us when we make our
requests, we also know that he will give us
what we ask for."

1 John 5:14–15

Jesus said that if I ask for anything in his name, he will do it.[1] He also said that if I keep on asking, then I would receive.[2] There is power in prayer, and here God promised that if I ask for something that pleases him, he will give it to me!

———•◆•———

Father, you said that there is great power in effective prayer.[3] Therefore, in response to your Word, I come boldly into your throne room of grace.[4] I ask, in the name of Jesus, for a wife to be brought into my life—a partner for life and ministry. I ask for my church to explode with growth and for prodigals to return to you. I ask that your bride—the Church—would wake up from her complacency and be revived with a burning passion for you. I ask for pastors to be filled with the fire of the Holy Spirit once again and to proclaim the truth of the Word of God boldly. I ask for revival on this land. Let a Third Great Awakening be upon us!

God, I know you hear and answer. I know these requests please you, so I eagerly wait to see how you will fulfill them.

DAY 53

HE IS ABLE

READ: JUDE 1

"Now all glory to God, who is able to keep you from falling away and will bring you with great joy into his glorious presence without a single fault."

Jude 1:24

What an incredible promise! Sometimes there is a great fear that I will mess up royally and destroy my relationship with God.

"I've messed up too much!"

"I've failed way too often!"

"Maybe I can't even be fixed."

"Maybe this addiction cycle is how life is going to be lived."

These were continuous thoughts when I was stuck in the PMO addiction cycle. Even after many days of freedom, there is the creeping thought of ruining it all.

The beauty of this verse is the promise that God can keep me from falling away! If I repent and return to God when I sin, he will pick me up, dust me off, and embrace me with his tender lovingkindness. He will empower me and remind me of who I really am. This is the encouragement I choose to focus on: now that I am on track, God can keep me on track! Then one day I will enter his presence in heaven and be with him forever!

———————◆•◆•◆———————

Father, thank you that you are able! You have kept me close to you even when I was doing dumb things in rebellion to you. Even when I didn't see it, you continually protected me from people who would have destroyed me. God, you have always been there. You won't let me fall away. I trust that you will keep me safe. I look forward to being with you in eternity!

DAY 54
FOOLISH PREACHING

READ: 1 CORINTHIANS 1

"Since God in his wisdom saw to it that the world would never know him through human wisdom, he has used our foolish preaching to save those who believe."

1 Corinthians 1:21

Preaching that Christ was crucified is a powerful thing. For most of the people I encounter, it is going to sound foolish. But to those whose hearts have been softened by the Holy Spirit, the Gospel will cut right through their souls to bring salvation. The Holy Spirit does not want me to worry about my natural ability to preach or developing "clever speech." Paul said that he feared clever speech would make the Gospel lose its power.[1]

So, I shouldn't be overly concerned with saying everything the right way or presenting a persuasive argument. If I did that, then it would have been me that won someone to Christ. People whom I share the Gospel with would look to me more than to the Lord. I don't want the credit or glory. I want God to get *all* the credit and glory! I want God's power to go out from my obedience to touch lives. I know with the Holy Spirit's help, this "foolish preaching" will change many people's eternity.

God, I want to be confident in the power of the Gospel when I preach. Fill me up, Holy Spirit! Help me be bold when I share your truth, and help me deliver your message of salvation with grace and love. I don't want to boast in my achievements or abilities. I only want to share what you tell me to say. It may sound foolish to some, but I will gladly sound foolish for you.

DAY 55
ONE PLANTS, ONE WATERS

READ: 1 CORINTHIANS 2-3

"We are only God's servants through whom you believed the Good News. Each of us did the work the Lord gave us... The one who plants and the one who waters work together with the same purpose. And both will be rewarded for their own hard work."

1 Corinthians 3:5, 8

There is a role that I play in spreading the Gospel and expanding the Kingdom of Heaven. Often, I don't know where people are with God when I meet them. There is the chance I may never see them again. That's why I must be faithful and try to plant the seed of truth into their hearts by preaching and teaching the Gospel. Regardless of how they respond, I know the seed has been planted.

Sometimes the seed of the Gospel has already been planted in the heart by someone else. My job then becomes to water that seed by supplementing it with the Gospel and the teachings of God's Word. Sometimes I get the amazing opportunity to reap the harvest of a person coming to Jesus and seeing real life change in him or her. What a joy and privilege that has been when I get to play that role!

No matter which role I play on a given day, my job is to be obedient, even if I don't see any results in a person's life. It is *God's* role to make the seed grow. I will be rewarded for my hard work whether I plant, water, or bring in a harvest.

———————◆•◆•◆———————

God, it can be very discouraging to see people not respond to the Gospel. Regardless, I want to be obedient to you. I will plant the seed when you say so. I will water it when you tell me. The goal is always the same: to bring people into a relationship with you and raise them up into Christ-like maturity. I choose today to be obedient no matter how someone responds.

DAY 56
THE POWER OF GOD
READ: 1 CORINTHIANS 4

"For the Kingdom of God is not just a lot of talk;
it is living by God's power."
1 Corinthians 4:20

aith is more than what I say. My faith must be
demonstrated through my actions; otherwise, it is
nothing more than a dead faith.[1] Some people may say all the
right things and have all the wisdom in the world, but what
do their lives look like? How are they living? Are they living
out the God life in all its fullness? It's easy to say that I believe
in God. It is another thing altogether to walk it out in humble
obedience to the Lord every day. Too often, people will claim
to know the truth, but by their actions, they prove that they
don't love God at all.[2]

I want my life to be more than just talk. I want my life to
be full of the power of God. I want my actions every day to be
an example of God's grace and mercy. I say that I love God,
so I want to live that claim out in complete obedience to him
and his Word.

Father, I recognize that true faith is not just words—it's living by your power. I don't want to just say that I love you. I want your power to flow through me every day so I can live an abundant life in you. I refuse to live a life of hypocrisy, so Holy Spirit help me as I strive to match my actions with my spoken beliefs. I want your name to be glorified through my life.

DAY 57
RUN!

READ: 1 CORINTHIANS 5-6

"Don't you realize that those who do wrong will not inherit the Kingdom of God? Don't fool yourselves. Those who indulge in sexual sin... or commit adultery, or are male prostitutes, or practice homosexuality... none of these will inherit the Kingdom of God... Run from sexual sin! No other sin so clearly affects the body as this one does. For sexual immorality is a sin against your own body."

1 Corinthians 6:9, 10, 18

Corinth was an idolatrous, sexually perverse, and pagan-worshiping city. Society today has a lot in common with Corinth. The Apostle Paul strongly urged that I should not deceive myself and become desensitized to the sins of the world around me. The people who "indulge"—regularly participate with pleasure—are not saved and will not go to heaven. The world may accept these practices, especially the sexual ones, but God does not. He does not change.

These actions are contrary to how I am designed by God and contrary to how I am supposed to live.

Therefore, I must *run* from sexual immorality in my life. Run in stark terror! Don't cozy up with or make allowances for it in my heart. I must stay away from sexual sin because it is corruption for my heart, mind, and body. I have felt this physical, mental, and emotional corruption from PMO. Sexual immorality only destroys my life. Thank God I have been set free, cleansed, and made holy by calling on the name of the Lord Jesus Christ![1]

———◆◆◆———

Father, the perverse sexual practices that are approved and commonplace in society are evil in your eyes. Participating in these acts only brings corruption to my body. No wonder you tell me to run from it! So that is what I commit to doing today. I will run from all sexual immorality, even if it's not popular with the culture or people around me. I will stand for truth. I commit my body, mind, and soul to you as a living sacrifice that is holy and pleasing to you!

DAY 58
LAYING DOWN MY RIGHTS
READ: 1 CORINTHIANS 8

"If what I eat causes another believer to sin, I will never eat meat again as long as I live— for I don't want to cause another believer to stumble."

1 Corinthians 8:13

Not all things are black and white. The Corinthian church asked the Apostle Paul a question concerning eating discounted meat from the supermarket that had been previously offered to idols. Some believers thought it was wrong to eat while others didn't see any issue. Who is right? Paul encouraged them to lay down their rights. The mature believer should lay down his rights to eat the discounted meat so that the younger, weaker believer's conscience isn't violated. Eating meat isn't worth causing someone to stumble.

In the same way, there are non-sinful things in my life that I have a freedom to do that might cause a younger Christian to stumble. For example, I have a freedom to eat cookies and ice cream because I have learned to eat it in moderation and for special occasions. But someone who is struggling with his health and weight may stumble if he sees me eating these desserts! It might influence him to consume them and make him feel guilty—or worse—like he was sinning! Therefore, if not eating desserts in front of him will keep him from stumbling, then I will gladly lay down my right to eat cookies and ice cream so that he can stand strong.

Father, extending grace to others isn't always easy, especially when it is over issues that don't violate my conscience. Give me the compassion I need to extend love to my brother or sister in Christ. Help me to show grace over the various issues of life. I choose to lay down my rights. I don't want to cause anyone to stumble by my "freedoms." Reveal to me, Holy Spirit, areas in my life where I can show more grace to others.

DAY 59
RUN TO WIN
READ: 1 CORINTHIANS 9

*"Don't you realize that in a race everyone runs,
but only one person gets the prize? So run to
win! All athletes are disciplined in their training... So I run with purpose in every step...
I discipline my body like an athlete, training
it to do what it should. Otherwise, I fear that
after preaching to others I myself might be
disqualified."*
1 Corinthians 9:24–26

Disciplined. Training with purpose. This describes an athlete who is focused on winning. The Apostle Paul compared my life of faith to an Olympic athlete. These Olympians would run completely naked so they wouldn't have any hindrances during their races. They disciplined their body to respond to the pressures of the sport. They trained hard so that they wouldn't be disqualified to win the grand prize.

What am I doing to be disciplined in my race of faith? The most important discipline is the habit of spending time with the Lord daily. It must be a part of my lifelong routine and cannot end! Maintaining an open communication with God through prayer is crucial, and I must continue to read the Bible so that I can know the truth. Only the truth I know will set me free.[1] I don't want to be disqualified by being ensnared once again to the lusts of the former life. So, to maintain freedom, I must privately meet with God daily. It is part of the training that I need.[2]

Holy Spirit, I refuse to be disqualified and veer off the course of faith. I don't want to become weary and give up. No! I will run hard and give it all I've got. I will do your will. Your Kingdom will be expanded. Lives will be transformed through your spirit working through me. Revival will come, and I will take part in it. I run to win!

DAY 60
A WARNING TO US

READ: 1 CORINTHIANS 10

*"These things happened to them as examples
for us. They were written down to warn us
who live at the end of the age."*
1 Corinthians 10:11

The stories of Moses leading the Israelites through the desert were written down as examples to warn me. But from what? Israel saw many miraculous signs and wonders, yet God was not pleased.[1] They were all cared for physically and spiritually, yet God was not pleased.[2] Why wasn't God pleased with them? They craved evil things and worshiped idols.[3]

What does the Lord consider evil? Sexual immorality, grumbling, complaining, and testing his authority.[4] These evil things are all rooted in idolatry. The Israelites craved to go back to Egypt because of the idolatry in their hearts. They did not want to worship God fully. They only came to God when it was convenient for them to have their needs met.

The warning to me is this: If you think you are standing strong, be careful not to fall.[5] I will face the same temptations as everyone else, including the Israelites. I will be tempted to test what God has said, to complain against him and his delegated authority, and to indulge in sexual immorality. I must choose to flee when I am confronted with the idols of sex and pride. I can't let anything become occupied in the altar of my heart other than Jesus Christ.

———————◆·◆·◆———————

God, I am not better than anyone else. I will be tempted like everyone else in the world. I choose to flee from the idols of sex and pride. I refuse to let any false god occupy the altar of my heart. I tear down anything that is worshiped other than you, Jesus. Holy Spirit, show me any idol that has taken root in my heart. I throw them down and refuse to worship anything or anyone other than you. Only you are worthy! I live to please and worship you alone!

DAY 61
THE GOAL OF GIFTS

READ: 1 CORINTHIANS 12-13

"So you should earnestly desire the most helpful gifts."

1 Corinthians 12:31

E verybody loves receiving gifts. Some people love giving gifts even more, and I think the Holy Spirit is in this category. During public worship services, the Holy Spirit desires to hand out spiritual gifts, or special abilities. The Apostle Paul wrote an overview about these spiritual gifts and explained how God knits the church body together to care for and help each other.[1] It does not say they are given to me to help *me* but to help *others*. Spiritual gifts are *others focused*. That is why Paul tells me to earnestly desire the most helpful gifts.[2]

This attitude of serving others in the church with spiritual gifts is firmly rooted in love. I could be able to speak in all the earthly and heavenly languages, prophesy, have special faith, be generous, or even face martyrdom, but without love fueling it all, it is annoying, unfulfilling, and worthless.[3] "Let love be your highest goal!"[4]

Yes, I should desire spiritual gifts, but these gifts are for ministering to others—they aren't for me. When I have a need, the Holy Spirit will give gifts to other people who then can minister to me. In this way, we can help each other and both be encouraged and built up.

Father, I desire your spiritual gifts. Use me to administer them to encourage, comfort, and strengthen people during worship services. Forgive me where I have sought these gifts only for myself. I want to serve you by serving others around me. Change my heart so that I can love them better and deeper. Whatever way you want to use me Lord, I am willing!

DAY 62
STRENGTHEN EVERYONE

READ: 1 CORINTHIANS 14

"When you meet together... everything that is done must strengthen all of you... be eager to prophesy, and don't forbid speaking in tongues. But be sure that everything is done properly and in order."
1 Corinthians 14:26, 39–40

What does God want church services to look like? During their services, the believers in Corinth were competitively yelling over each other in tongues, and the women, who sat on the opposite side of the room, were interrupting the services by shouting questions to the men. I bet their services were wild! Paul concluded his teaching on spiritual gifts by explaining how to have an orderly worship service. The believers were to be respectful and take turns sharing their gifts.[1] Yes, they were to eagerly desire spiritual gifts, especially prophecy, and they were not to forbid someone from speaking in tongues. But everything in church had to be done decently and in order.[2]

My modern church services may look different, but God still wants them to be in order! This doesn't mean they have to be boring or stiff, and it doesn't mean that I should neglect or forbid spiritual gifts. But it does mean my church services should have some sort of schedule and order. When the Holy Spirit shows up, everything will flow together properly.

———————•◦•◆•◦•———————

Lord, you said that I should desire the special gifts and abilities the Holy Spirit gives to the church, especially the gift to prophesy. My desire now is for all the gifts of the Holy Spirit to be operational in my life. I want to be used in the supernatural realm where, by the power of your Spirit, I can lay hands on the sick, and they will recover. I want to give a word of knowledge or wisdom to speak truth into someone's life. I desire to have special faith to believe for a miracle or an outpouring of your presence. Here I am, Lord! Use me to minister to your Church!

DAY 63
WHAT IS MOST IMPORTANT
READ: 1 CORINTHIANS 15

"Let me now remind you, dear brothers and sisters, of the Good News I preached to you before... I passed on to you what was most important... Christ died for our sins, just as the Scriptures said. He was buried, and he was raised from the dead on the third day, just as the Scriptures said."

1 Corinthians 15:1, 3–4

This is what is most important: the Gospel. Jesus died for my sins, and then defeated death by being raised to life on the third day. Paul mentioned "the Scriptures" twice without quoting them. Which ones was he referring to?

The first is Isaiah 53. This is a beautiful prophecy about the Messiah taking all my punishment, all my sins, all my diseases, and all my rebellion. Verse 11 says, "Because of his experience, my righteous servant will make it possible for many to be counted righteous, for he will bear all their sins." Jesus Christ bore all these things on the cross so I could be healed and forgiven to be in a love relationship with him.

The second is Psalm 16:10: "For you will not leave my soul among the dead or allow your holy one to rot in the grave." Jesus connected his death and resurrection to Jonah being in the belly of the fish for three days and three nights.[1] Even though Christ would be killed for my sins, he wouldn't remain dead. No, God would not allow his son to rot in hell; Jesus would defeat death by his resurrection.[2] Through faith in him, I have received victory over sin and death![3]

———•◦◆◦•———

Thank you, Jesus, for the sacrifice you made for me on the cross. Because I believe in your death and resurrection, I am declared righteous before you. I am healed and made whole. I have eternal life, and I have a home in heaven. Death was defeated, and sin no longer has any power over me. God, give me the strength and boldness to share this Good News. Lord, guide me into opportunities to proclaim your goodness. I want to tell people the most important thing this world has ever known.

DAY 64
REMOVED, REVEALED, REFLECTED
READ: 2 CORINTHIANS 2-3

"So all of us who have had that veil removed can see and reflect the glory of the Lord. And the Lord—who is the Spirit—makes us more and more like him as we are changed into his glorious image."

2 Corinthians 3:18

What causes people to not see the truth of the Gospel? Paul said one reason is that there is a hardness over the minds of unbelievers, so they can't understand the truth. There was a time when this veil was over my mind and heart. I didn't understand the Gospel fully. I had not fully understood the depth of how much I had sinned against God and how desperately I needed a savior to rescue me from the grips of sin.

This changed when the Holy Spirit convicted my heart to see my need for him.[1] Since I surrendered my life to Christ in faith, that veil was removed, and God's glory was revealed to me. I now have the honor and privilege to come boldly into God's presence and meet with him.[2] As I meet with him in his presence, I begin to look more like Christ. I am changed into his glorious image, and his glory shines in my life. As a result, my life becomes a reflection of God's glory and presence to the world.

———•◆•———

Thank you, God, that I can come boldly into your presence. Holy Spirit, I ask for you to continue to reveal more of yourself so I can reflect your glory to the world. Let me be a shining light to others in this dark and crooked world. Lord, I also ask for you to remove the veil over the minds of unbelievers so they too can experience your forgiveness and grace.

DAY 65
A NEW LIFE HAS BEGUN

READ: 2 CORINTHIANS 4-5

"Either way, Christ's love controls us. Since we believe that Christ died for all, we also believe that we have all died to our old life. He died for everyone so that those who receive his new life will no longer live for themselves. Instead, they will live for Christ, who died and was raised for them... This means that anyone who belongs to Christ has become a new person. The old life is gone; a new life has begun!"

2 Corinthians 5:14-15, 17

My entire motivation for living has changed! Christ became my sin so that I can be made right with God.[1] Because I believed this, I don't have to pay the penalty of my sin.[2] Christ was raised for me, so I could experience eternal life. Before Christ came into my life, my motivation was to live for myself, but now I want to live for Christ. My purpose in life shifted from living for my wants and desires to living for his.

I now pursue the things he loves and hate the things he detests. It's no longer me living, but Christ living in and through me.[3]

Yes, because I belong to Jesus, I live for him. I have become a new creation, a new person. My old, sinful life is dead. Now, I have eternal life. I am saved and set free.

God, thank you for making me into a new person. This is who I really am. You have paid the price for my sins. They are completely gone! My record is completely wiped clean! Now my nature is godly, and my motivation is to please you. God, I choose to line up my life with the reality of my transformation. The old life is gone, and the new has come!

DAY 66
COMPLETE HOLINESS
READ: 2 CORINTHIANS 6:1-7:4

"Don't team up with those who are unbeliev-ers. How can righteousness be a partner with wickedness? How can light live with darkness?"
2 Corinthians 6:14

I f anyone experienced hardships, it was the Apostle Paul. It's encouraging to read of the fruit that was produced in him and his ministry team despite the troubles they faced. Even when facing persecution or opposition from political or religious leaders, they remained faithful.[1] Paul knew firsthand the importance of having the right people on your team. That's why I think Paul encouraged the Corinthians to not part-ner with unbelievers. The Corinthian church had "withheld [their] love from [him]."[2] Instead of partnering with Paul and his team, they seemed to have partnered with unbelievers. Paul was opposed to this due to opposing worldviews and morals.

Partnering with people who have opposing ideologies will only bring trouble into my life. If I am going to be effective at sharing the Gospel like the Apostle Paul, I must surround myself with a team of believers who have the same mind and spirit.[3]

God declares that he will live in and walk among me since I am a temple of his Holy Spirit. This motivates me to become holier so I can be more effective in my service to God. Therefore, I must choose a righteous lifestyle and to surround myself with people who are pursing the same goal.

Father, I commit to only partnering with those of the same mind and mission in marriage, ministry, and every other area in my life. My desire is to be a gold utensil for a special purpose;[4] therefore, I aim for holiness. Holy Spirit, expose anything in my life that may defile me so I can get rid of it.[5] I commit myself to live a life separate and pure before you.

DAY 67
GODLY SORROW
READ: 2 CORINTHIANS 7:5-16

*"For the kind of sorrow God wants us to expe-
rience leads us away from sin and results in
salvation. There's no regret for that kind of
sorrow. But worldly sorrow, which lacks repentance, results in spiritual death."*
2 Corinthians 7:10

There is no doubt that my sorrow towards PMO had
been worldly. I had never gotten to the place where it
was truly godly sorrow. Godly sorrow produces a true change
of mind and direction in life. That was not my experience.
I became accustomed to my sin and had begun to enjoy and
love it. Yet I also hated it because I knew it was wrong. My
life was plagued by a constant cycle of sin, guilt, shame, and
confession. Lather, rinse, and repeat. What a miserable man
I had become![1]

The breakthrough was during my initial TRF interview.
As I shared my struggle, I felt the sorrow of my sin and wept.
The weight of continuing in my sin was too much to bear any
longer. Enough was enough. Repentance was solidified when

I shared my decision to join TRF with my pastor that same afternoon. Godly sorrow led to godly repentance which led me away from my sin. I don't regret that pain. I don't regret that sorrow. Look at what this godly sorrow and repentance produced in me![2] My relationship with God is stronger than ever before. I've found healing for my emotional wounds, and I have rediscovered the truths of God's Word. My life has never been the same!

God, words can't describe how grateful I am that you never gave up on me. I am so thankful that I finally experienced godly sorrow that led to a complete change of mind. You orchestrated the events in my life so that I could find freedom from my addiction and sin. Holy Spirit, I want to thank you for this freedom with my life. It is in complete service to you. I am all yours! Take me wherever and use me however you choose. God, I am willing!

DAY 68
GENEROUS LIVING
READ: 2 CORINTHIANS 8-9

"Remember this—a farmer who plants only a few seeds will get a small crop. But the one who plants generously will get a generous crop... 'For God loves a person who gives cheerfully.' And God will generously provide all you need. Then you will always have everything you need and plenty left over to share with others."
2 Corinthians 9:6, 7-8

G odly people are generous people. In fact, those that are spiritually mature are usually the most generous people I know. Not only are they generous with their finances but with their time and service as well. Jesus also modeled this for me. "You know the generous grace of our Lord Jesus Christ. Though he was rich, yet for your sakes he became poor, so that by his poverty he could make you rich."[1] This isn't just financially; it is spiritually rich.

God has called me to live a generous life. Since Jesus generously gave his life, I should be generous with mine through my finances, time, and service. I should be an investor into the Kingdom of God and people. Jesus said to "store up [my] treasures in heaven, where moths and rust cannot destroy,"[2] and "where [my] treasure is, there [my] heart will be also."[3] What I invest in continually is what I will be passionate about. I want to be passionate about seeing people enter the Kingdom of God. Living a generous life like Jesus did will help this be fulfilled.

———————◆•◆•◆———————

Jesus, you were generous throughout your life on earth, and the climax was when you gave up your life for me and all humanity. Help me to live a lifestyle of generosity every day. Show me the resources I have so that I can bless and help others in need. As I do this, I know I won't have to worry about my own needs, for you will provide all I need.

DAY 69
BIG GOD

READ: ISAIAH 40

"O Jacob, how can you say the Lord does not
see your troubles? O Israel, how can you say
God ignores your rights?"

Isaiah 40:27

L ife can be tough at times. Some days it seems like I am surrounded by problems, and it can feel overwhelming. Disappointments, inner wounds, and the stresses of everyday life can weigh me down and leave me extremely discouraged. After God dealt with her sins, the nation of Israel found herself in a similar situation. The people needed comfort and encouragement, so God said to the prophet Isaiah, "Comfort my people."[1]

How did Isaiah comfort Israel? He reminded them of the greatness of God: God holds the ocean in his hand, measures the skies with his fingers, and knows the weight of the earth and all the mountains.[2] The earth is like a grain of sand to God.[3] No offering is big enough,[4] no nation is great enough,[5] and no image or idol is glorious enough to compare to the Lord.[6] He created all the stars in the universe, and he calls every one out by its name.[7] Considering all this, God asked Israel, "How can you say the Lord does not see your troubles?"

———•••◆•••———

God, thank you for giving me perspective on my life and problems. You do see my problems! You do care about how I feel and what I am going through! Those who trust in you can receive strength from you,[8] so I choose today to trust in you. I refuse to trust in my own wisdom, the wisdom of others, or the wisdom of world. My trust is in you alone. Thank you for seeing me! Thank you for renewing me! I give you everything!

DAY 70
REAL AUTHORITY
READ: MARK 1:1-28

"The people were amazed at his teaching, for he taught with real authority—quite unlike the teachers of religious law."

Mark 1:22

The teachers of that day often quoted what the commentators or esteemed teachers thought about the Scriptures. Jesus didn't need to consult with anyone; he was the very Word of God himself![1] Jesus came into this church meeting and taught what the Scriptures meant with *authority*. He knew the heart of the Word because he *was* the heart of the Word.

God has called me to preach and teach the Word of God with authority. This authority can't come from my own knowledge and wisdom, and it can't come from what other teachers or Bible commentators have said either. It must come from God. While studying the Bible and gaining knowledge is important, the authority must come from above. Jesus said that all power and authority have been given to me by him over the enemy.[2] So with the Holy Spirit's anointing, I know that I will

151

proclaim God's Word to overcome the kingdom of darkness and to advance the Kingdom of God.

———————•◆•———————

Holy Spirit, I know that as I continue to study the Bible, you will reveal truth to me. I don't want to proclaim your truth with just knowledge. I need your authority. A Great Awakening is underway, and I want to be used to advance your Kingdom. Here I am, Lord Jesus. Use me! Give me great boldness in preaching your Word. Stretch out your hand with healing power and let miraculous signs and wonders be done through the name of Jesus Christ![3]

DAY 71
DIRECTION FROM PRAYER

READ: MARK 1:29-45

"Before daybreak the next morning, Jesus got
up and went out to an isolated place to pray."
Mark 1:35

J esus modeled for me the importance of getting away to
pray. *When* he got away to pray is very interesting. Jesus
got up early "before daybreak." This was probably when no
one else was awake so he could focus on the Father in prayer.
During this time of prayer, I believe Jesus received direction
for his ministry. A move of God had occurred in Capernaum
and many people were healed. Even though Jesus' fame was
increasing in the city, he had determined to move forward
towards other towns.[1] Great things were happening in Capernaum, but Jesus knew he could not stay there.

This goes against what I would naturally believe is right.
If people were flocking to Jesus and hungry for God, doesn't
it make sense to stay and minister to them? Yet Jesus left the
town. This is a great example of why spending time with God
in prayer must be important for me. When will I know when I
need to stay? When will I know when I need to move forward?

Only God can give me those directions, so I must seek him in prayer to clearly hear those instructions.

———◆———

Lord, spending time early in the morning with you is important and meaningful. I know you will speak to me and give me clear directions for my life. No matter what is going on, I choose to seek you in prayer and Bible study daily. I need your guidance and strength more than ever. Draw closer to me as I draw closer to you.[2]

DAY 72
SIGNS AND WONDERS
READ: MARK 2:1-3:19

"Then he appointed twelve of them and called them his apostles. They were to accompany him, and he would send them out to preach, giving them authority to cast out demons."

Mark 3:14–15

Everywhere Jesus went, people experienced healing. Leprosy was cleansed, blind eyes were opened, sicknesses were cured, demons were cast out, and physical deformities were restored. Jesus anointed his twelve apostles to do the same things. They were given authority to not only preach the Gospel but to cast out demons and to heal all diseases.[1]

Before Jesus ascended to heaven, he said that those who believe would be able to place their hands on the sick, and they would be healed.[2] I know I will see these types of miracles again in my life, and God will use me to administer these gifts to people.[3] Revival is coming. The preaching of the Gospel will once again be confirmed by signs and wonders: miracles, healings, demonic exorcisms, salvations, infillings of the Holy

Spirit, and broken strongholds. I want to see these things. I *know* I will see them in my life.

----●●◆●●----

Father, I ask for the same powerful anointing that was upon the twelve apostles to be upon my life. You have given me a message to preach. I know that as I proclaim the Gospel, you will confirm it through signs and wonders. Bondages will be broken, and devils will be cast out of people's lives. Listeners of the Gospel will be released from their hurts and pains. Physical maladies will disappear.

But none of this is possible apart from you. I must "accompany" you, Lord Jesus, through it all. Apart from you, I can't do anything,⁴ so Holy Spirit, fill me up! Consume me with your holy fire and use me to further your Kingdom in this coming revival.

DAY 73
BIND THE STRONG MAN

READ: MARK 3:20-35

"Who is powerful enough to enter the house
of a strong man and plunder his goods? Only
someone even stronger—someone who could
tie him up and then plunder his house."

Mark 3:27

Many of the teachers of religious law refused to believe that Jesus was the Son of God. If Jesus' authority and power didn't come from God, then where? "He's possessed by Satan, the prince of demons. That's where he gets the power to cast out demons," the religious leaders exclaimed.[1] In response to this, Jesus illustrated that he was more powerful than Satan! Who can overpower someone as powerful and strong as the devil? Only someone more powerful can bind him up and rescue those whom he has enslaved.

The authority of Jesus and the power from the Holy Spirit have been given to me as well.[2] In the name of Jesus, I can take authority over the enemy to stop acting and conducting evil in people's lives. Without the Holy Spirit, I am powerless over the enemy,[3] but with the authority and power of Jesus, there is overwhelming victory![4]

———————◆•◆•◆———————

Lord Jesus, you have given me the authority of your name to cast out demons and to lay hands on the sick. You said that what I bind on earth will be bound in the heavens.[5] Therefore, in your authority, I bind up the enemy's activity in my life. I bind up the enemy's activity in my friends' and family's lives. I bind up the enemy's activity in my nation's affairs. Holy Spirit, open the eyes of those who can't see the truth. Awaken their hearts and souls to understand the gravity of their sin and their need for you. Bring revival to this land!

DAY 74
PAY ATTENTION
READ: MARK 4

"Pay close attention to what you hear. The closer you listen, the more understanding you will be given—and you will receive even more. To those who listen to my teaching, more understanding will be given. But for those who are not listening, even what little understanding they have will be taken away from them."
Mark 4:24–25

What am I listening to? What I listen to will influence me. Jesus is challenging me to pay attention to what I hear, so I must listen to the truth. What is the truth? It's the teachings of Jesus; he *is* truth![1] Listening isn't just hearing, it's doing. I must apply and obey the teachings of Jesus. When I listen to and obey the truth, I will receive more revelation from the Holy Spirit. As a result, I can be more effective in living out my faith and spreading the Gospel.

Jesus also gives me a warning: If I don't listen to his words and apply them, then I will lose out on experiencing the life God wants me to live. Deception can creep into my life, and

I will backslide in my relationship with God. I will lose the knowledge and understanding that I had once before. Therefore, I must be influenced by the truth, not what is coming out from news outlets, social media, or the government. It's the words of Jesus that bring life and maturity into my life. I must listen to them!

———————◆•◉•◆———————

God, I want to always be good, fertile soil. I want to continually grow in your grace and your Word. As I read the Bible, I ask that you keep revealing your truth to me. Show me applications for my life. Holy Spirit, I want to live out my faith effectively, so equip me to do it. I choose today to not just listen but apply your teachings.

DAY 75
A DIFFERENT REACTION
READ: MARK 5:1-20

*"And the crowd began pleading with Jesus to
go away and leave them alone."*
Mark 5:17

This is a very different reaction to what happened
earlier in Capernaum. There, after Jesus cast out a demon
during the synagogue service and healed Peter's mother-in-law,
the whole town gathered to watch as "many sick and demon
possessed people were brought to Jesus."[1] After seeing the
demon-possessed man healed, the people of Gerasenes begged
for Jesus to go away and leave them alone. Two very different
reactions to miracles.

Once the Holy Spirit begins to move again through signs,
wonders, and healings, some people will be drawn closer to
Jesus. Their curiosity will give them an opportunity to hear
and witness the power of God and the Gospel of Jesus Christ.
The results will be like in Jesus' day. Some will embrace the
power of God and the Gospel. They will choose to surrender
their lives to Christ and be saved. Others will reject it all. In
this story, "they were all afraid."[2] Something about God's power

made them scared to approach him. Fear caused them to push Jesus away and reject the Gospel.

———————◆◆◆———————

Lord, there are people in the world who are hungry and in desperate need of you. I pray that you would lead me to those who, like in Capernaum, are drawn to the Gospel to be saved and healed. I know I will encounter some who will reject the Gospel out of fear. Help me not get discouraged when this happens. Holy Spirit, give me the strength to stay focused on scattering the seed of truth[3] and rejoice with those who choose you in faith.

DAY 76
JUST HAVE FAITH
READ: MARK 5:21-43

*"But Jesus overheard them and said to Jairus,
'Don't be afraid. Just have faith.'"*

Mark 5:36

aith is the main element and requirement for healing. Someone must demonstrate faith in God for it to manifest. An example of faith for healing is in Jairus' statement to Jesus: "Please come and lay your hands on her; heal her so she can live."[1] Jairus was desperate. No doubt he had seen or heard about the miracles Jesus had performed. Jairus demonstrated his faith by traveling to the shore to meet and plead with Jesus to come heal his daughter. His faith was activated and confirmed by his actions.[2]

Jairus further demonstrated his faith on the journey home with Jesus. When the report came that his daughter was dead, Jesus replied, "Don't be afraid. Just have faith."[3] Jairus didn't give up on his daughter when the report came. He listened to Jesus and continued the journey home with him. As a result, he experienced not only the healing but the resurrection of his daughter! Sometimes a bad report may come, but I must keep believing that God is doing a good work. A miracle is on the way. Healing will happen. I can't become overwhelmed with fear. Fear kills faith.

———————◆•◆•◆———————

God, I pray that you will increase my faith. I want to be like Jairus and run to you immediately when I need help for myself or others. Lord, increase my faith so that I can have full confidence in you to heal when I ask. Even when bad reports come, help me to stand firmly in my faith in you. I refuse to allow fear to overtake my mind anymore. Fear will not conquer my faith. I choose to trust in you!

DAY 77
UNBELIEF

READ: MARK 6:1-13

"Because of their unbelief, he couldn't do any miracles among them except to place his hands on a few sick people and heal them."

Mark 6:5

U nbelief is demonstrated in many forms. In Gerasenes, it manifested in *fear*.[1] Because they were afraid, Jesus didn't perform many miracles. Their fear closed themselves off from receiving healing. In Nazareth, unbelief manifested in *scoffing* and *offense*. The people scoffed at Jesus' teachings. Why would they scoff at the preaching of truth, repentance, and the Kingdom of God? Maybe they thought things like this: "How can Jesus, the carpenter's son, call us out? We know him! What right does he have to preach to us like this?" Because of their familiarity with Jesus, they scoffed at his teachings and were offended. They refused to believe in him.[2]

I have seen people do this today. As I have tried to share the Gospel, people have scoffed at me. They refused to believe in Jesus Christ. I have been mocked and ridiculed for believing in the outpouring of the Holy Spirit[3] or the operation of spiritual gifts.[4] Sadly, the result is that these people do not see many miracles among them due to their unbelief.

———————◆•◆•◆———————

Father, help me in my unbelief. I don't want to fear. I want to have faith in my life. Forgive me where I have demonstrated fear and scoffed at the miraculous. Forgive me where I have developed an offense against you. I choose today to have faith in you and in your Word. What you said and did before will happen again in my lifetime! Give me the faith I need to believe for the miraculous!

DAY 78
WATCH YOUR MOUTH
READ: MARK 6:14-29

"Then the king deeply regretted what he had said; but because of the vows he had made in front of his guests, he couldn't refuse her."
Mark 6:26

My mouth can get me into trouble. It sure did for Herod. He spoke too quickly because he was caught up in the moment of his party. He was distracted and mentally intoxicated by the lustful dances of Herodias' daughter. Herod's lust and pride overtook his rational mind, and he made a reckless mistake that cost the life of John the Baptist. The Bible speaks often about being slow to speak[1] and even when to speak at all.[2] I must be careful with what I say!

Herod also caved to the political pressures around him. "Because of the vows he made in *front of his guests*, he couldn't refuse her." Herod cared more about power and advancement than doing what was right. The political pressures of the situation overcame him. Everyone has a choice on how to respond to the situations and temptations of life. Herod could have easily refused her request, but he did not. He could have changed the parameters of his vow. After all, he was the top official over the region, but he did not. Herod buckled under political and social pressure, and it cost the life of someone else.

Lord, I look at the example of Herod as a warning to watch what I say. I want to be a man of uncompromising integrity, even if that means I must upset other people or risk my reputation to others. Even if there is great personal cost to me, I will do and say what is right in your sight!

DAY 79
THEY DIDN'T UNDERSTAND
READ: MARK 6:30-53

"They were totally amazed, for they still didn't understand the significance of the miracle of the loaves. Their hearts were too hard to take it in."
Mark 6:51-52

In the middle of a powerful storm, the disciples were rowing hard and struggling against the wind and waves.[1] They were terrified as they watched Jesus walk across the lake. As he approached the boat, Jesus proclaimed who he was: I AM.[2] The disciples were speechless when the storm calmed. "You really are the Son of God!" they exclaimed.[3] The disciples were shocked because they failed to understand the power within Jesus. They didn't understand this miracle because they didn't understand the significance of the previous one: the miracle of the loaves.

What was the importance of this miracle? Jesus, who is the Son of God, is also the one who can do all things! He provided exactly what the crowd and the disciples needed by supernaturally multiplying food. Jesus bypassed all the natural laws of the earth. This miracle was a sign to the disciples that God would take care of them. The power of God shown through Jesus earlier that day should have increased their faith to trust him to get them through the storm. They missed out on what God was doing now because they didn't understand what God had done before.

Are there things that God is doing around me that I don't understand because my heart is too hard? Do I miss out on the power of what God is doing now because I don't understand what God did before? Could previous miracles be a lesson to increase my faith for the current move of God?

————◆•◆•◆————

Lord, I want to recognize you for who you are—the I AM. Reveal to me where you are working because I want to join you. Lead me and guide me according to your will. I want my heart to be soft and pliable so I can understand what you are doing. Remind me of the miracles you have done in the past so I can recognize the miracles of today. What you did before, you will do again!

DAY 80
THE HEART

READ: MARK 7

"It's not what goes into your body that defiles you; you are defiled by what comes from your heart."

Mark 7:15

The heart is the most important thing to the Lord. The Pharisees and other religious leaders were doing all the right things on the outside, but they were ignoring the corruption within their hearts. In another place, Jesus called them white-washed tombs—pretty and clean on the outside but dead and decaying on the inside.[1]

Whatever manifests into my life stems from my heart. The issues I face, the temptations I fall for, and the reactions I make all come from what is in my heart. Jesus said, "For from within, *out of a person's heart*, come evil thoughts, sexual immorality, theft, murder, adultery, greed, wickedness, deceit, lustful desires, envy, slander, pride, and foolishness."[2] If any of these things appear in my life, then there is an issue in my heart that needs to be confronted. Something needs to be uprooted.

God, search my heart and point out anything that offends you.[3] Show me the issues in my heart that need to be confronted and uprooted. I don't want these things to defile me or hinder my relationship with you or others. Holy Spirit, continually cleanse me! Expose these evil and sinful thoughts and actions so that I can remove them. My desire is to be pure and holy before you.

DAY 81
SKEPTICS
READ: MARK 8

"When the Pharisees heard that Jesus had arrived, they came and started to argue with him. Testing him, they demanded that he show them a miraculous sign from heaven to prove his authority."

Mark 8:11

Another sign of unbelief is *skepticism*. The Pharisees were skeptical of Jesus' ministry. No doubt they, like so many others, had heard of the demons expelled, eyes opened, legs strengthened, and tongues loosed. Despite all the works of Jesus they encountered, they didn't respond in desperation and faith like the Syrian woman.[1] These religious leaders were skeptics and refused to believe. They argued with Jesus in pride instead of begging for mercy in humility.[2] As a result, Jesus declared, "I will not give this generation any such sign."[3] He left the region without performing any miracles! Jesus didn't argue with the skeptics. He spoke the truth, and then moved on to places where people were hungry for the truth.

———————◆•◆•◆———————

Lord, I don't want to be like the Pharisees and be skeptical of the miraculous. I want to see signs and wonders. I know they are coming, and I know you will show your mighty hand once again. The blind will see, the deaf will hear, and the dead will be raised to life in the name of Jesus. You promised that I will lay hands on the sick, and they will recover.⁴ Regardless of my experience, I refuse to be skeptical. I choose today to believe your Word.

DAY 82
SHAKY FAITH
READ: MARK 9:1-29

"'Have mercy on us and help us, if you can.'
'What do you mean, 'If I can'?' Jesus asked.
'Anything is possible if a person believes.'
The father instantly cried out, 'I do believe,
but help me overcome my unbelief!'"
Mark 9:22–24

ircumstances can have profound impacts on faith. A father brought his son to Jesus' disciples to be healed from an evil spirit. His faith appeared to be strong initially, but the miracle didn't come as expected. The disciples prayed, but the child did not get well. This seemed to damage the father's faith. Now, instead of bringing his son to Jesus in confidence, he had shaky faith: "Help us, *if you can.*"[1]

Shaky faith is another form of unbelief. It appears as genuine faith, but there is an uncertainty to it. It looks like faith on the outside, but the foundation is doubt. Being timid or providing God an escape clause to a request for healing does not bring a miracle. If I want to see healing in my life, then I must believe with my whole heart. Jesus replied to the father, "Anything is possible *if a person believes.*"[2] In another place, Jesus said that I can pray for anything, but I must truly believe and not have any doubt in my heart. If I have faith, then what I ask for will be mine.[3]

Father, I know my faith has been chipped away from not seeing miracles happen as I expected. However, my cry today is the same as the father: "Help me overcome my unbelief!" I want to believe for healings and miracles with expectancy. I want to see it. I want to see you move again. Holy Spirit, restore my heart to complete confidence in you. I choose to believe healings will occur in other's lives and mine.

DAY 83
LAST PLACE

READ: MARK 9:30-50

"Whoever wants to be first must take last place
and be the servant of everyone else."
Mark 9:35

W ho is the greatest? This is an argument that came up often among the disciples. When confronted by Jesus, they were embarrassed and didn't reply. Jesus used this opportunity to describe the greatest in the Kingdom of God: "Whoever wants to be first must take last place and be the servant of everyone else."

Servants are in last place because they humble themselves among their peers.[1] They embrace and love children.[2] They perform miracles in the name of Jesus to bring the Father glory.[3] Servants are hospitable and help others with their physical needs.[4] To Jesus, the servant is the greatest in the Kingdom of God.

What is causing me to not humble myself and take last place? Is there anything hindering me from being a servant to others? If so, then I must get rid of it![5] The motivations behind my actions need to be checked because they will be tested by the Lord.[6] God has called me to preserve this world with good works and enhance it by living as a servant to Jesus and others. Therefore, I can't allow anything to keep me from being a humble servant.

Father, you said that the greatest in the Kingdom of God is a servant, so I choose today to take last place and serve others. I humble myself before you. Help me to see what people need. Whether the need is physical, emotional, or spiritual, Holy Spirit, please provide the resources to meet it. Use me to be the salt of the earth so that your name can be praised and glorified![7]

DAY 84
BLIND FAITH

READ: MARK 10

"Jesus said to him, 'Go, for your faith has healed you.' Instantly the man could see, and he followed Jesus down the road."

Mark 10:52

B artimaeus was just a blind man sitting along the roadway when an encounter with Jesus completely changed his life. He heard Jesus coming down the road, so he desperately cried out to him for mercy. Jesus had Bartimaeus brought to him and asked a very interesting question: "What do you want me to do for you?"[1] Couldn't Jesus see the man was blind? Jesus knew Bartimaeus was blind, but he was looking for a faith response. Bartimaeus could have asked for many things: food, money, or clothes. He could have demanded justice and for Jesus to rebuke those who had ignored and abandoned him. Yet Bartimaeus didn't ask for these material things. He asked for his sight!

Bartimaeus had blind faith. He believed he was healed even before he received the miracle. This man's faith was in action. If I want to see the miraculous in my life, then I must recognize Jesus for who he is—the Messiah. Like Bartimaeus, I know God can touch me, so I must speak out my requests in faith. Then I can experience the same words the formerly blind man heard: "Go, for *your faith* has healed you."[2]

Lord, I recognize who you are—the Son of the living God. You are the one who died for my sins and offered forgiveness to me and the entire world.[3] You do not change.[4] You are the same yesterday, today, and forever.[5] You have healed in the past, you heal now, and I know you will heal in the future. Therefore, I ask in faith for you to bring healing to my mind and body, in the name of Jesus. I ask in faith for healing for those I know who are sick and suffering from disease. Holy Spirit, use me to administer your gift of healing. Let me encounter people who need a touch from you. What you did before, I know you will do again!

DAY 85
IT WILL BE YOURS
READ: MARK 11

*"I tell you, you can pray for anything, and if you
believe that you've received it, it will be yours."*
Mark 11:24

What an amazing promise! I can pray for anything and
receive it by faith, but there is a condition to this
promise. Jesus was speaking to his disciples. He previously said,
"If any of you wants to be my follower, you must give up your
own way, take up your cross, and follow me."[1] As a disciple, I
have denied my desires and live for what God desires. I have
died to the old sinful life. I'm now living the resurrection life
empowered by the Holy Spirit. I am following Jesus and his
purposes and ways. In doing this, the motivation behind my
prayers is lined up with God's heart. I am not living for myself
but for the glory of God and to further his Kingdom. So, when
I make a request to him, I can ask in faith and believe I have
already received it. Then, I wait with patient expectancy for
God's answer to my prayers to become a reality in my life.

———•◆•———

God, you promised that I can pray for anything and receive it by faith. I want this to be a reality in my life, so I choose to completely align myself as your disciple. I lay down my selfish desires so that I can live for what you desire. I cut off any connection with my old life so that I can live the God life. I refuse to follow the ways of culture. I want to follow the ways of the Kingdom of God. Holy Spirit, I ask now for boldness to request big things in the name of Jesus, for with faith, nothing is impossible for you.[2]

DAY 86
THE MISTAKE

READ: MARK 12

"Your mistake is that you don't know the Scrip-
tures, and you don't know the power of God."
Mark 12:24

In the final week of his ministry, Jesus was tested many
times by the religious leaders. They were determined to
trap, arrest, and find ways to kill him.[1] In one instance, the
Sadducees tried to trap Jesus with a strange hypothetical story
and question. But Jesus wasn't thrown off by this. He simply
pointed them back to the truth found within the Scriptures.

It's easy to get caught up in strange theories and "what ifs"
about the Bible. The Apostle Paul warned Timothy to avoid
endless discussions of myths and spiritual pedigrees that only
lead to controversies. These things only raise questions in
people's minds and don't help them live a life of faith.[2] I have
encountered many who have tried to involve me in endless
discussions about hypothetical scenarios or endless meanings
of words.[3] The mistake with focusing on these things is that
it can lead someone off course in their walk with God. When
I encounter these situations, I want to do what Jesus did with

the Sadducees: point them back to the truth found within the Scriptures.

———•◦◆◦•———

Holy Spirit, help me to have discernment when people ask me about the Bible. Show me the motive behind every question. I want to follow your example, Lord Jesus, so help me respond in grace, authority, and truth. I don't want to be fearful of these situations, so I ask for courage and boldness. Give me the wisdom whether to engage in a conversation or let it go.

DAY 87
THE FUTURE
READ: MARK 13

"No one knows the day or hour when these things will happen, not even the angels in heaven or the Son himself. Only the Father knows. And since you don't know when that time will come, be on guard! Stay alert!"
Mark 13:32–33

Jesus gave me a blueprint of what will happen in the end times. False teachers will be rampant and deceive many people. Wars between nations will take place. Natural disasters and famines will occur in many parts of the world. Jesus compared these signs to birth pains. As a mother gets closer to giving birth, labor pains become more frequent and intense.[1] This is how it will be in the last days.

There is no doubt the world is becoming more corrupt every day. Crime, hatred, and immorality are rampant. The culture is constantly pulling people further from Christian values and principles. Even though life is intensifying, the good news is that Jesus is returning! He will be back for his bride. While I wait, I am to be on guard,[2] stay alert,[3] and watch for him.[4]

God has also given me instructions about the work I am to do during this waiting period—preach the Gospel and advance the Kingdom of God.⁵ Until Jesus' return, I will do this!

———————◆·◆·◆———————

Lord, I want to be ready for your return. You are coming soon for your church.⁶ Then, you will discipline the people of Israel and those remaining on the earth.⁷ While I wait for your return, use me to bring others into your Kingdom. I want people to escape the coming judgment on the world and an eternity in hell. Give me boldness to be your ambassador and to proclaim the Gospel.

DAY 88
KEEP WATCH AND PRAY
READ: MARK 14

"When he returned to them again, he found
them sleeping, for they couldn't keep their
eyes open. And they didn't know what to say."
Mark 14:40

Jesus was approaching what would be the hardest night and day of his entire life. His entire mission for coming to earth would be accomplished within hours. The weight of what was to come was overwhelming, so Jesus longed for his closest friends to be there to pray with him. He told the disciples to "pray so that you will not give in to temptation"[1] and to "keep watch with me."[2]

What were the disciples to be on the lookout for? Was it for the coming mob? The devil? Jesus wanted them to be on guard physically and spiritually for what was to come. He was about to be arrested, and they were all going to be tested in their faithfulness and loyalty to him. They needed strength to not give in to the temptations of fear, worry, or anger. Yet they didn't know what to pray, and they slept. The lack of purpose in their prayer time led to weariness and falling asleep.

There have been times in my life when God asked me to keep watch and pray, and all I did was sleep. I didn't know what to pray, and I became tired. Because I didn't pray with purpose, I wasn't equipped to handle the temptations in my life. Jesus wants me, like the disciples, to keep watch and pray so I won't give into temptation. This is the key: To stand firm against the attacks of the enemy, I must pray with purpose. I must be aware. I must keep watch.

———◆◆◆———

Father, help me stay awake to pray and keep watch! I want to be aware and prepared for the temptations that come in my life. Holy Spirit, I need your power to do your will. My spirit is willing, but my body can be weak and fail. Fill me up with your strength so that I can keep watch and pray. I ask for an urgency to rise in my spirit to passionately pray with power and purpose.

DAY 89
PROPHECY

READ: ZECHARIAH 12-13; MARK 15

*"They will look on me whom they have pierced
and mourn for him as for an only son. They
will grieve bitterly for him as for a firstborn
son who has died."*

Zechariah 12:10

The prophet Zechariah predicted many things concerning the Messiah and the future age. Hundreds of years before Jesus walked the earth, God declared "they will look on *me* whom they have pierced."[1] The prophet prophesied by the Spirit of God that *God himself* would be pierced and mourned. This was completely fulfilled when the people of Israel would look at Jesus on the cross as he died for the sins of the world. Many would mourn over his death, but "on that day a fountain will be opened... to cleanse them from all their sins and impurity."[2]

Jesus' sacrifice paid the price to cleanse humanity from all their sins and impurity. Everything I had ever done was washed over by the blood poured out by God! By believing in the death and resurrection of Jesus, my sins were forgiven![3] Everything the prophets predicted came true!

God, you gave the prophets glimpses of your plan of redemption. You laid out details for them, and then fulfilled it all in Jesus Christ. This was all planned out by you so that I could be adopted into your family forever.[4] You planned long ago that I could be cleansed and forgiven of my sins. Your Word is unshakable and true. I praise you, God!

DAY 90

THE COMMISSION

READ: MARK 16

*"Go into all the world and preach the Good News
to everyone. Anyone who believes and is bap-
tized will be saved. But anyone who refuses to
believe will be condemned. These miraculous
signs will accompany those who believe: They
will cast out demons in my name, and they will
speak in new languages. They will be able to
handle snakes with safety, and if they drink
anything poisonous, it won't hurt them. They
will be able to place their hands on the sick,
and they will be healed."*

Mark 16:15–18

Lord, as I finish reading the Gospel account, I am so
thankful for your sacrifice. Because your blood was shed,
I *am* healed. Because your body was broken, I *am* forgiven.[1]
Thank you for forgiving and cleansing me of all my sins. Thank
you for saving my life. I was heading toward hell, but you
reached down and took hold of me.[2] You rescued me from all
my pains, hurts, and addictions. You exchanged my past for a

brand-new life,[3] and you have planned my future.[4] Your words are my life,[5] so I thank you and worship you!

Lord Jesus, use me to further your Kingdom. Fill me and anoint me with power and boldness of the Holy Spirit to be a witness for you. My life is yours! You have commissioned me as a believer, disciple, and solider of Christ. Therefore: I will preach the Good News! I will speak in tongues and cast out demons! I will handle snakes safely and drink poison without worry! I will lay hands on the sick, and they will be healed!

CONCLUSION

"[God] heals the brokenhearted and binds up their wounds [healing their pain and comforting their sorrow]."

Psalm 147:3 AMP

The greatest discovery during my time in *The Retention Formula* was the root issue to my addiction to pornography. During my conversation with Gianfranco on Instagram, I was asked why I thought I kept returning to pornography. The question caught me off guard. I couldn't come up with an answer! It turns out it was much deeper than being bored or stressed.

I had hurts and wounds in my heart dealt by my mom.

As I mentioned in the Introduction, my parents divorced when I was young. At eight years old, it was difficult to process the reality that Mama and Daddy were no longer married. Life was going to look a whole lot differently. My dad was incredibly supportive growing up. He was, and still is, a terrific father. My dad sacrificed so much to raise my sister and me the best way he knew how. I never questioned his love or commitment to us.

My mom's story is quite different. She lived a very selfish life and often chose to live out her pleasures and desires instead of being present and raising her children. There were many times where she would decide to leave birthday parties, holiday gatherings, or Sunday dinners to be with her friends instead of spending time with her family. During the divorce period, she left my sister and me at our grandmother's house for several days without informing my dad. Repeated instances like this made me very calloused towards her, and I stopped caring for a long time. I could only process so much rejection and abandonment. This suppression didn't help me emotionally, and it only fueled my PMO addiction.

At some point, my mom got involved with drugs and alcohol. What started as an addiction to pain medications and social drinking led to illicit drug use and alcoholism. These addictions destroyed what little relationships she had remaining with her family. She rejected me, time after time, to spend time with friends associated with her addiction. The drug and alcohol use also destroyed my mom's body and mind. The years of abuse to her body led to many hospitalizations, one of which put her on a ventilator in the ICU for several days. We thought she was going to die, but she miraculously pulled through and was released from the hospital just a few days after she woke up. Over time, my mom's heart became so weak from overdose episodes that she eventually suffered from a lethal heart attack.

Life with my mom was filled with event after event where I experienced emotional pain and stress from being abandoned and rejected by her. Every time I tried to give her another chance to rebuild our relationship or reach out to help her when she was in need, she would soon reject and abandon me again for her own selfish desires like she had done when I was a child.

One morning during my devotionals, I felt impressed by the Holy Spirit to write down all the major instances that I could recall where I had experienced rejection in my life. It took a while, but as I wrote down every scenario I could remember, I began to see the pattern: I felt the most drawn to pornography when I felt abandoned or rejected by others, especially the people I cared about the most. I never realized, until God showed me during this devotional while in TRF, that I had been using pornography to mask the pain of abandonment, rejection, and loneliness in my life that had started when I was nine or ten years old. Because this started so early in life, it became a stronghold in my mind.

Every time those same emotions would resurface, I was drawn to pornography. In a sense, PMO became my own drug to numb the hurts and pains in my heart. I discovered that what I really needed was not something to put a band-aid over my wounds, not something to numb my feelings, and not something to stuff the thoughts to the side.

I needed healing.

I needed God to come in and bring restoration to my mind and emotions. I needed God to heal my hurts. I needed God to patch up my wounds.

An incredible thing happened at the end of my soul-searching survey. God began to touch these damaged areas of my life. The psalmist declared that "[God] heals the brokenhearted and binds up their wounds [healing their pain and comforting their sorrow]."[1] He showed me through his Word that I am not abandoned—for God says that he will never abandon or forsake me.[2] He showed me that I am not rejected but chosen by him to be a part of his family.[3] He showed me the people in my life that truly love and care about me. As the presence of God filled me, I knew my heart was being healed. Because of this healing work of Jesus Christ in my life, I know that I am completely free from the addiction of PMO that plagued my life for over two decades.

Friend, where are you today? Is your heart in need of healing? The good news is that no matter where you are in life, you aren't too far gone from God. He wants to restore your life. He wants to heal your heart.

It all begins with being in a love relationship with God. Where do you stand with Jesus Christ today? Are you confident that if you died today that you would go to heaven? I encourage you to settle the matter today. Surrender your life to Christ! The Bible declares that "if you openly declare that Jesus is Lord and believe in your heart that God raised him from the dead, you will be saved. For it is by believing in your heart that you are made right with God, and it is by openly declaring your faith that you are saved."[4]

Salvation is a gift that we cannot earn or deserve. The Apostle Paul made this clear when he said, "Salvation is not a reward for the good things we have done, so none of us can boast about it."[5] It is only by believing in the death and resurrection of Jesus Christ that you are saved. You must choose to receive Jesus into your life.

To receive this gift, you must first acknowledge your sin before God. To sin means to miss the mark. We've all done that, and pretty badly. The Bible tells us that "everyone has sinned; we all fall short of God's glorious standard."[6]

Secondly, you must choose to repent of those sins. Repentance means to go in the other direction with a complete change of mind. It's the choice to walk away from living for yourself and Satan to living your life for Jesus and his Kingdom. The Bible says to "repent of your sins and turn to God, so that your sins may be wiped away."[7]

Finally, you must choose to receive Jesus Christ into your life. Will you do that today? If you would like to start, or recommit to, a real, living relationship with Christ, simply pray this prayer and sincerely mean it:

———————◆———————

"Lord Jesus, I know that I am a sinner. I believe that you came down to this earth to take the capital punishment I deserve for my sins. I believe you paid my debt when you died on the cross, and I believe you were raised back to life in three days.

Right now, I choose to turn away from my selfish and sinful life, and I choose to follow you, Jesus. Come into my life as my Savior, my Lord, and my God. I choose to live my life, with your help and to the best of my ability, to honor you. Thank you for giving me brand new life. Amen."

NOTES

INTRODUCTION
1. Proverbs 26:11
2. Romans 7:15. 18–21, 24

DAY 5
1. Galatians 5:1 AMPC
2. Ibid.
3. Romans 6:6
4. Galatians 5:24
5. Romans 12:1

DAY 6
1. Galatians 6:4
2. Matthew 25:21; Luke 19:17

DAY 8
1. Ephesians 1:3
2. Ephesians 1:4
3. Ephesians 1:5
4. Ephesians 1:11
5. Ephesians 1:14

DAY 9
1. 2 Corinthians 5:17

DAY 10
1. See James 1:2–4

DAY 11
1. See Romans 12:2

DAY 12
1. Ephesians 1:5
2. Ephesians 5:3
3. Romans 12:1

DAY 13
1. John 10:10
2. Colossians 2:15
3. James 4:7

DAY 14
1. Philippians 1:5
2. Philippians 1:7
3. Philippians 1:12
4. Philippians 1:14
5. Philippians 1:18
6. Philippians 1:27

DAY 15
1. 1 Peter 2:11
2. John 14:2
3. Philippians 1:27
4. Philippians 2:2
5. Philippians 2:4
6. Philippians 2:5–11
7. Philippians 2:15
8. Philippians 2:22
9. Colossians 1:13

DAY 16
1. Philippians 3:6; Acts 8:3
2. Acts 8:1
3. Hebrews 12:1–2

DAY 17
1. As quoted often by Gianfranco Martinez in *The Retention Formula*.
2. James 1:22

DAY 19
1. Romans 6:6
2. Romans 6:16

DAY 22
1. Ephesians 1:5

DAY 24
1. 1 Thessalonians 4:4
2. Romans 6:16

DAY 25
1. 1 Thessalonians 4:16–17
2. 1 Corinthians 15:51–53
3. Psalm 145:11–13; Daniel 7:14; Revelation 20:4; Revelation 22:3
4. 1 Thessalonians 5:2; 2 Peter 3:10; Revelation 3:3; Revelation 16:15
5. 1 Thessalonians 5:6

DAY 26
1. John 15:5
2. Matthew 19:26
3. Philippians 4:12

DAY 27
1. 1 Corinthians 15:33

DAY 28
1. 1 Timothy 1:19

DAY 29
1. 1 Timothy 3:2
2. 1 Timothy 3:4
3. 1 Timothy 3:2, 6
4. 1 Timothy 3:3
5. 1 Timothy 3:6
6. 1 Timothy 3:3

DAY 30
1. 1 Corinthians 6:19

DAY 31
1. Romans 12:2

DAY 33
1. 2 Timothy 3:14
2. 2 Timothy 4:2

DAY 34
1. 2 Peter 1:3
2. Philippians 2:13
3. John 8:31–32 AMPC

DAY 35
1. Romans 5:1 HCSB
2. 2 Corinthians 5:17 MSG
3. Ephesians 1:5

DAY 36
1. Luke 15:11–31
2. Hosea 2:6–7
3. 2 Corinthians 4:4

DAY 37
1. Hebrews 3:19
2. Hebrews 3:8
3. Hebrews 3:10
4. Hebrews 4:3

DAY 39
1. 1 Timothy 2:4
2. Ephesians 5:27

DAY 40
1. 1 Corinthians 6:18; Ephesians 5:3; Colossians 3:5; 1 Thessalonians 4:3
2. 2 Timothy 2:21

DAY 42
1. Hebrews 11
2. Hebrews 12:1
3. Hebrews 12:2
4. Matthew 26:39

DAY 43
1. Ephesians 1:5

DAY 44
1. 1 Peter 1:4
2. 1 Peter 1:13
3. 1 Peter 1:13–15
4. 1 Peter 1:22
5. Ibid.
6. 1 Peter 1:23–2:1

DAY 46
1. John 16:33
2. Matthew 10:42; Luke 6:22; John 15:19
3. Matthew 6:11
4. John 15:18
5. James 1:2
6. Acts 5:41

DAY 47
1. 2 Corinthians 5:11
2. 2 Peter 1:9 TLB
3. Matthew 7:24–25

DAY 48
1. 2 Peter 2:3
2. 2 Peter 2:2, 13–14, 18
3. 2 Peter 2:18–19
4. 2 Peter 3:9

DAY 49
1. John 14:21, 23
2. 1 John 2:4; James 1:22

DAY 50
1. 1 John 3:24
2. 1 John 3:6, 9
3. 1 John 3:15, 17
4. 1 John 3:14, 18

DAY 51
1. 1 John 5:1
2. Ephesians 1:5
3. Colossians 1:13
4. Colossians 2:15
5. Zechariah 2:10–12; Zechariah 8:3; Zechariah 14:9–10; Revelation 20:6
6. 2 Corinthians 4:4
7. John 16:33

DAY 52
1. John 16:23-24
2. Matthew 7:7-8
3. James 5:16
4. Hebrews 4:16

DAY 54
1. 1 Corinthians 1:17

DAY 56
1. James 1:14, 17
2. Matthew 7:15–20; 2 Timothy 2:5; Titus 1:16

DAY 57
1. 1 Corinthians 6:11

DAY 59
1. John 8:31–32
2. 1 Timothy 4:8

DAY 60
1. 1 Corinthians 10:1–2
2. 1 Corinthians 10:3–5
3. 1 Corinthians 10:6–7
4. 1 Corinthians 10:8–10
5. 1 Corinthians 10:12

DAY 61
1. 1 Corinthians 12:7
2. 1 Corinthians 12:31
3. 1 Corinthians 13:1–3
4. 1 Corinthians 14:1

DAY 62
1. 1 Corinthians 14:29–35
2. 1 Corinthians 14:40 ESV

DAY 63
1. Matthew 12:40
2. 2 Timothy 1:10; Hebrews 2:9;
   Hebrews 2:14; Revelation 1:18
3. 1 Corinthians 15:57

DAY 64
1. John 16:8
2. Hebrews 4:16

DAY 65
1. 2 Corinthians 5:21 PHILLIPS
2. Romans 3:24
3. Galatians 2:20

DAY 66
1. 2 Corinthians 6:7–8
2. 2 Corinthians 6:12
3. 1 Corinthians 1:10;
   Philippians 2:2; 1 Peter 3:8
4. 2 Timothy 2:20–21
5. 2 Corinthians 7:1

DAY 67
1. See Romans 7:14–24
2. 2 Corinthians 7:11

DAY 68
1. 2 Corinthians 8:9
2. Matthew 6:20
3. Matthew 6:21 NIV

DAY 69
1. Isaiah 40:1
2. Isaiah 40:12
3. Isaiah 40:15
4. Isaiah 40:16
5. Isaiah 40:17
6. Isaiah 40:18–20
7. Isaiah 40:26
8. Isaiah 40:31

DAY 70
1. John 1:1
2. Luke 10:19
3. Acts 4:29–31

DAY 71
1. Mark 1:38
2. James 4:8

DAY 72

1. Luke 9:1
2. Mark 16:18
3. 1 Corinthians 12:9
4. John 15:5

DAY 73

1. Mark 3:20
2. Mark 3:1, 16:17
3. See Acts 19:13–16
4. Romans 8:37
5. Matthew 18:18

DAY 74

1. John 14:6

DAY 75

1. Mark 1:32
2. Mark 5:15
3. Mark 4:14

DAY 76

1. Mark 5:23
2. James 2:20 PHILLIPS
3. Mark 5:36

DAY 77

1. Mark 5:15
2. Mark 6:3
3. See Acts 1:8, 2:1–40
4. See 1 Corinthians 12–14

DAY 78

1. James 1:19
2. Proverbs 15:28, 26:5–6, 29:20

DAY 79

1. Mark 6:48
2. Mark 6:50
3. Matthew 14:33

DAY 80

1. Matthew 23:27
2. Mark 7:21–22
3. Psalm 123:23–24

DAY 81

1. Mark 7:24-29
2. Mark 8:26
3. Mark 8:12
4. Mark 16:18

DAY 82

1. Mark 9:22
2. Mark 9:23
3. Mark 11:23–24

DAY 83

1. Mark 9:35
2. Mark 9:36–37
3. Mark 9:39
4. Mark 9:41
5. Mark 9:42–48
6. Mark 9:49
7. Matthew 5:13–16

DAY 84

1. Mark 10:51
2. Mark 10:52
3. Isaiah 53:4–6; John 3:16
4. Malachi 3:6
5. Hebrews 13:8

DAY 85

1. Mark 8:34
2. Matthew 17:20, 19:26; Mark 10:27; Luke 18:27

DAY 86
1. Mark 11:18, 12:12–13
2. 1 Timothy 1:4
3. 1 Timothy 6:4

DAY 87
1. Matthew 24:4–12
2. Mark 13:32
3. Ibid.
4. Mark 13:36
5. Mark 13:34
6. Revelation 3:16
7. Daniel 9:24

DAY 88
1. Mark 14:38
2. Mark 14:34

DAY 89
1. Zechariah 12:10.
2. Zechariah 13:1
3. John 3:16; Romans 10:9–10
4. Ephesians 1:5

DAY 90
1. Isaiah 53:4–6
2. Psalm 18:16
3. 2 Corinthians 5:17
4. Jeremiah 29:11
5. Deuteronomy 32:47

CONCLUSION
1. Psalm 147:3
2. Hebrews 13:5
3. Ephesians 1:11
4. Romans 10:9–10
5. Ephesians 2:9
6. Romans 3:23
7. Acts 3:19

ACKNOWLEDGMENTS

*"Friends love through all kinds of weather, and
families stick together in all kinds of trouble."*
Proverbs 17:17 MSG

Writing a book has always been a dream of mine, but
I never imagined that it would be fulfilled. This has
been one of the most rewarding things I have ever experienced.
None of it would have been possible without the love and
support from so many people around me.

I want to thank my pastors, Greg and Lisa. Pastor Greg, you
have been the greatest example of Jesus to me. Your encouragement and support throughout my life has meant the world.
When I thought I was disqualified, you saw potential. Thank
you for investing your life into mine. I will always love
being your Timothy.

Pastor Lisa, thank you for being "Mama" when I desperately
needed a mother figure in my life. I know I can come to you
with anything for any reason. I love you, and I'm so proud to
be called your "son from another one."

I also want to thank my dad, Rusty. Daddy, the sacrifices
you made raising Shana and me were not unnoticed by either
of us or by God. The work the Lord has done in our family is

truly remarkable. Thank you for always being such a consistent figure in my life. It means the world to me. I love you.

To my sister, Shana: you have been an integral part of my life. We have traversed a lot in our lives, and I'm thankful you've been there the whole way. I'm proud to have you as not only as a sister but as a friend. I love you so much.

To my brother-in-law, Micaiah: Thanks so much for the amazing cover artwork you and Shana did. It turned out beautifully, and I couldn't be more pleased. Thanks for all you've done for me over the years. I'm glad you are part of the family.

To my friends. To Hope: You were one of the first people I pitched this book idea to. Thank you for letting me bounce all my ideas off of you while we were supposed to be working out at the gym. Your encouragement and support throughout this entire writing process continually helped fuel the fire to persevere to the end. My life is enriched by your friendship. Thanks for everything.

To Amanda: Our early talks of writing books were what made it possible for me to believe I could do something like this. Thanks for being an incredible friend. I can't wait to write together someday.

To Brandon and Bradley: You are truly "iron sharpens iron" kind of men. Anytime I am around you, I am encouraged and strengthened. The passion and hard work you have poured into your music inspired me to complete this book. Thank you for your integrity and commitment to the Lord. We're going to change the world.

To the others I consider close in my life: Beth, Tiff, Noah, Mandy, Christy, Nick, and Sharon. You all play a vital role in my life, and I'm blessed to call you all family. I appreciate your love, support, and encouragement more than I could ever express.

To the TRF community. To Gianfranco: Thank you for allowing yourself to be used by God to create *The Retention Formula*. Your willingness to use your experience to help hundreds of guys like me find freedom from PMO honors and pleases God. I know you'll have a great reward in heaven one day for your service. Without TRF, I would likely still be bound, and this book would never have been created. God bless you, my friend.

To Coach Rye: I appreciate all your encouragement while I was going through the program, whether it was said directly to me or to others during a coaching call. You're doing a great work, and I appreciate all your support.

To Brant: Thank you for writing the book blurb. It captures the essence of the book beautifully.

Thank you to my beta readers: Debra and Julian. I appreciate all the feedback and recommendations to the manuscript. Your input made this better than I could have done alone.

Finally, and certainly not least, I want to thank God. Lord Jesus, thank you for walking with me through this process all these years and bringing healing to my heart during my time in TRF. My life has been revolutionized because of the powerful work you have done in my mind and soul. Words can't describe all the thanks in my heart. I am nothing without you, and my life is forever yours. May this book be used to bring you glory.

ARE YOU STRUGGLING WITH PORNOGRAPHY?

You can join the same program that helped Joel Vaught find freedom from pornography.

For more information about *The Retention Formula*, connect with Gianfranco on Instagram: @gianfrancomartinezez

Ready to join the program? Visit this link and use the code "JOELV" at checkout to get 50% off your first month!

https://bit.ly/TheHealedHeart

ABOUT THE AUTHOR

Joel Vaught currently serves as an associate pastor in Conway, SC. He also serves as a recurrent chaplain at Adult & Teen Challenge in Georgetown, SC, and is passionate about people finding freedom in Christ. His life is centered around preaching the Gospel and seeing people thrive in their relationship with Jesus. Family and friends are an important part of his life as well as staying fit in the gym. *The Healed Heart* is his first book, and he hopes to reach many with life-changing truths from the Bible and his own experiences.

You can connect with Joel on Instagram @joelvaughtbooks or on Facebook at facebook.com/joelvaughtbooks. You can also visit his website, joelvaught.com.